Adventures + Co
Beginning
237 0151

P9-BYG-727

1·2·3
Reading & Writing

Pre-Reading and Pre-Writing Opportunities
for Working With Young Children

Written by Jean Warren

Illustrated by Marion Hopping Ekberg

Totline® Publications
A Division of Frank Schaffer Publications, Inc.
Torrance, California

VILLA PARK PUBLIC LIBRARY

Totline Publications would like to thank the following people for their contributions to this book: Betty Ruth Baker, Waco, TX; Kimberly L. Bateman, Downingtown, PA; Jana Burk, Kent, WA; Marjorie Debowy, Stony Brook, NY; Cindy Dingwall, Palatine, IL; Ruth Engle, Kirkland, WA; Rita J. Galloway, Harlingen, TX; Diane Himplemann, Ringwood, IL; Joan Hunter, Elbridge, NY; Melode Hurst, Grand Junction, CO; Barbara H. Jackson, Denton, TX; Ellen Javernick, Loveland, CO; Susan A. Miller, Kuztown, PA; Susan M. Paprocki, Northbrook, IL; Susan Peters, Upland, CA; Diana Shindler, Bay City, TX; Betty Silkunas, Lansdale, PA; Jane M. Spannbauer, So. St. Paul, MN; Marie Wheeler, Tacoma, WA; Nancy C. Windes, Denver, CO.

Editorial Staff:
   Gayle Bittinger, Kathleen Cubley, Brenda Lalonde, Elizabeth McKinnon
Production Staff:
   Manager: Eileen Carbary, *Assistant:* JoAnna Haffner
   Design: Kathy Kotomaimoce
   Computer Graphics: Carol DeBolt, Sarah Ness, Eric Stovall

©1992 by Totline® Publications. All rights reserved. Except for the inclusion of brief quotations in a review, no part of this book may be reproduced or utilized in any form or by any means, electronic or mechanical, including photocopying, recording, or by any information storage and retrieval system, without written permission from the publisher.

ISBN 0-911019-47-2

Library of Congress Catalog Number 91-65932
Printed in the United States of America
Published by: Totline® Publications
Editorial Office: P.O. Box 2250
                        Everett, WA 98203
Business Office: 23740 Hawthorne Blvd.
                        Torrance, CA 90505

20 19 18 17 16 15 14 13 12 11 10 9 8 7 6 5

Introduction

1·2·3 Reading & Writing is basically a two-part book, designed to be used as a language resource by teachers and parents of young children. The first section contains activities that develop pre-reading and pre-writing skills. The second section centers around opportunities for encouraging actual or simulated reading and writing.

As with all the books in Totline's 1·2·3 Series, *1·2·3 Reading & Writing* is filled with open-ended, no-lose activities. It offers opportunities for children to develop language skills through situations that are fun and anxiety free, yet meaningful to each child.

Pre-Reading and Pre-Writing Section

This section is made up of the first four chapters in the book — "Getting Ready to Write," "Getting Ready to Read," "Vocabulary Building" and "Alphabet Letters." These chapters contain a selection of activities that teach skills children need to develop before they can successfully learn to read and write, such as eye-hand coordination, visual discrimination, oral expression and letter recognition. (A number of the activities teach both pre-reading and pre-writing skills but are included in just one chapter to avoid repetition and confusion.) The more non-threatening experiences children have with these pre-reading and pre-writing skills, the easier time they will have when actually learning how to read and write.

Opportunities for Reading and Writing Section

Children learn best when they are immersed in situations that have meaning for them and when they are allowed to freely experiment without fear of failure. In this section of the book, you will find suggestions for providing environments and materials that naturally encourage children to "read" and "write." (Very young children will probably play-act reading and writing, while older children may actually try using beginning reading and writing skills.) Following are some points to keep in mind as you work with the activities in this section.

- When setting up reading and writing environments, let your job be to facilitate — not dictate — action.

- Make sure that all reading and writing activities are perceived by your children as having value, or as having relevance to their lives.

- Remember that before children can become readers, they need to understand the meaning of print and why it is an important part of people's lives.

- When introducing beginning reading to your children, be sure to use materials that allow them to grasp whole meanings rather than fragmented ideas.

- Try always to provide your children with environments in which they want to write because they have something to say or in which they want to read because there is something they want to know.

Opportunities to teach pre-reading and pre-writing skills are all around us. We as teachers and parents need only be aware of these opportunities and incorporate them naturally into the lives of our children.

Jean Warren

Contents

Getting Ready to Write

- ◆ **Pre-Writing Coordination Activities**
- ◆ **Writing Tools and Surfaces Activities**

Working With Playdough

Use the following recipe (or any favorite recipe) to make playdough. In a large bowl stir together 1 cup salt, 1 cup warm water and a small amount of powdered tempera paint or food coloring. Add 2 tablespoons vegetable oil and gradually stir in 2 cups flour. Work the dough with your hands, letting the children help. Add more flour or water if the dough feels too sticky or too dry. Give each child some of the playdough to poke, pound, squeeze and twist. Encourage the children to roll their playdough into snakes and small balls. Then set out small pans, table knives, potato mashers and other kitchen utensils for the children to use while working with their playdough.

Hint: Store the playdough in the refrigerator in an airtight container. It should last for two or more weeks.

Fingerpainting

Let the children fingerpaint on large pieces of butcher paper with a mixture of liquid starch and powdered tempera paint. Have them spread the mixture all over their papers with their hands. Then encourage them to fingerpaint designs by using their hands in different ways. For example, have them try painting with their fingertips, with their fingers pressed out flat, with their palms, with the sides of their fists and with their knuckles. For added fun, let the children dance their hands and fingers to music while they are working.

Variation: Let the children fingerpaint directly on a washable tabletop with shaving cream, hand lotion or a mixture of Ivory Snow soap powder and water.

Playing With Small Toys

Provide the children with opportunities to play with small plastic animals, people and cars. Set up environments that encourage the children to manipulate the toys in various ways. For example, place sand in a shallow box and let the children create scenes in the sand for their small toys. Or make a doll house by taping several open boxes together and placing spools, blocks and other small objects inside for furniture. Or use felt-tip markers to draw a map of a play town on a sheet of butcher paper or vinyl cloth. Tape the map to the floor and let the children have fun moving their small toys around on it.

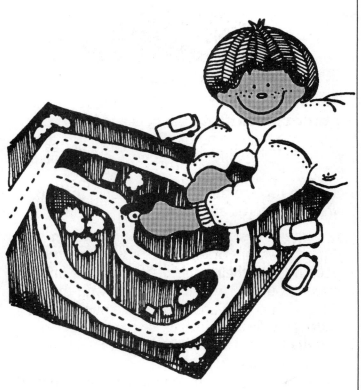

Clipping Clothespins

Tie a clothesline between two chairs. Set out a box of spring-type clothespins and a basket of fabric squares or clothing shapes cut from fabric. Let the children take turns using the clothespins to clip the fabric shapes to the clothesline.

Variation: Make a clothespin color wheel for the children to play with. Cut a 12-inch circle out of white posterboard and divide it into four or eight sections. Color each section a different color. Collect four or eight spring-type clothespins and color them to match the sections on the color wheel. Let the children take turns clipping the clothespins around the edge of the wheel on the matching colored sections.

Screwing on Jar Lids

Collect various sizes of plastic jars that have lids. Place the jars and the lids in a box. Let the children take turns matching the lids to the jars and screwing them on and off. As each child finishes playing, encourage him or her to return the jars and lids to the box so that they will be all together for the next person.

Screwing Nuts and Bolts

Purchase an assortment of large nuts and bolts that fit together. Take the nuts and bolts apart and place them in a box. Set out the box and let the children take turns screwing the nuts on the bolts and then unscrewing them. Have the children replace the nuts and bolts in the box when their turns are over.

Hint: Wipe the nuts and bolts with bar soap to make screwing them together easier.

Tearing Paper

Plan activities for the children that involve tearing paper. For example, let them tear pages cut from newspapers, magazines and catalogs just for the fun of it. Or guide them by asking questions such as these: "Can you tear a tiny piece of paper? Can you tear a huge piece of paper? Can you tear a long strip of paper? Can you tear a short strip of paper?" Or give the children strips of different colored construction paper and have them tear the strips into small squares. Use the squares later for a mosaic art project.

Variation: Let the children tear papers that have different patterns and textures, such as wrapping paper, wallpaper, sandpaper, tissue paper, aluminum foil, waxed paper and paper towels. Save the pieces for making collages.

Cutting Paper

For a beginning cutting activity, give each child a pair of blunt scissors and a strip of paper about one inch wide. Show the children how to hold and manipulate their scissors. Then let them practice snipping their paper strips into small pieces.

Extension: When the children are ready to try other cutting experiences, let them choose wallpaper samples or squares of wrapping paper to cut into pieces any way they wish. Or give them scraps of construction paper to cut into thin shapes, fat shapes, long shapes, short shapes, etc. Save the paper pieces to use for art activities.

Fun With Spoons

Let the children practice lifting and transferring different kinds of materials with spoons. For example, place a plastic measuring cup and a set of measuring spoons in a sandbox (or a box filled with cornmeal). Let the children take turns spooning the sand into the cup. Or have the children use teaspoons to transfer such things as rice or dried beans from one bowl to another.

Using Tweezers and Tongs

Plan activities that involve the use of tweezers and tongs. For example, put some O-shaped cereal pieces on a plate and set out a pair of tweezers. Let the children take turns picking up the cereal pieces with the tweezers and placing them on another plate. Or set out a small box and a pile of cotton balls. Have the children use a pair of kitchen tongs to pick up the cotton balls and put them into the box.

Extension: Encourage the children to look around the room for other small items and try picking them up with the tweezers or tongs.

Playing With Snap Beads

Set out a basket of large plastic snap beads and let the children have fun snapping them together and pulling them apart. If desired, have the children sort the beads by color before snapping them together. Or start color patterns by snapping several beads together and let the children continue the patterns. Encourage them to count the numbers of beads they snap together before they pull them apart.

Pegboard Games

Let the children play with commercial pegboard games. Or use sturdy shoeboxes with lids to make your own games. Punch small holes in rows in the shoebox lids. Place a number of different colored golf tees in each box. Let the children take turns inserting the golf tees into the holes in the shoebox lids any way they wish. Or let them use the tees for creating color patterns or for playing matching and counting games.

Jigsaw Puzzles

Make simple jigsaw puzzles for the children to piece together. Cut several 3- by 6-inch cards out of posterboard. If desired, cover one side of each card with colored or patterned self-stick paper. Cut each card into two interlocking puzzle pieces, making sure that each puzzle fits together differently. Then set out the pieces and let the children take turns putting the puzzles together.

Variation: Make jigsaw puzzles out of seasonal shapes cut from posterboard, picture postcards or magazine pictures that have been mounted on heavy paper and covered on both sides with clear self-stick paper.

Shape Puzzles

On a large plastic foam food tray draw several different geometric shapes (or trace around several different shaped cookie cutters). Carefully cut out the shapes with a craft knife. Make handles for the cutouts by folding strips of heavy paper in half, folding up the ends and gluing them to the tops of the shapes. Set out the food tray and the cutouts. Let the children take turns placing the cutouts into the appropriate holes in the food tray.

Variation: Collect several identical sponges and cut a different shape out of the center of each one. Place the shapes and the sponges in a box. Let the children take turns fitting the shapes into the matching holes in the sponges.

Building With Blocks

Set up an area in your room for block play. Provide the children with blocks of various kinds and sizes to use for stacking and building. Encourage play by stacking blocks in various ways and asking the children to make matching stacks. Or start building a block house and let the children take turns adding blocks to complete it.

Extension: Use half-gallon milk cartons to create your own blocks. To make each block, cut the tops off of two cartons. Wash the cartons thoroughly and allow them to dry. Stuff one of the cartons with crumpled newspaper. Then slide the top of the other carton over the top of the first carton and tape securely around the outside edges. Make as many blocks as you wish.

Designing With Popsicle Sticks

Have the children sit on the floor several feet apart from one another. Give each child a handful of Popsicle sticks. Let the children have fun arranging the sticks on the floor any way they wish to create designs, patterns or simple shapes.

Variation: Cut large squares out of heavy paper. On each square trace around a Popsicle stick to make the outline of a simple shape such as a square, a triangle, or a house. Set out the squares along with a box of Popsicle sticks. Let the children take turns placing the sticks on top of the tracings on the paper squares.

Carpentry Fun

Let the children enjoy the fun and challenge of sawing and hammering. Set up a small carpentry area which can be supervised at all times. Supply it with pieces of softwood, small sturdy saws and hammers, and nails with wide flat heads. If desired, include a sawed-off section of a tree trunk for the children to pound nails into.

Variation: For an activity that requires less supervision, let the children use toy hammers to pound wooden golf tees into thick pieces of plastic foam.

Toothpick Sculptures

Cut plastic foam into small pieces and give each child some toothpicks. Let the children fasten the foam pieces together with the toothpicks to create such things as animals, people, cars and trains. Later, the toothpicks and foam pieces can be pulled apart and used to create new sculptures.

Variation: For a snacktime activity, let the children make toothpick sculptures with vegetable chunks, cheese chunks or defrosted frozen peas. (Note: Have the children remove the toothpicks before eating their sculptures.)

Stringing Necklaces

Cut a number of plastic straws into 1- to 2-inch pieces. Give each child an 18-inch piece of yarn with a straw section tied to one end and the other end taped to make a "needle." Let the children string the remaining straw sections on their yarn pieces. Then tie the ends of each child's yarn piece together to create a necklace.

Variation: Instead of straw sections, use wooden beads, dried pasta shapes or *O*-shaped cereal pieces. For necklaces that can be strung and restrung in different ways, give the children long shoelaces that have been knotted at one end and buttons that have large holes.

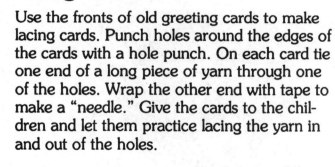

Lacing Cards

Use the fronts of old greeting cards to make lacing cards. Punch holes around the edges of the cards with a hole punch. On each card tie one end of a long piece of yarn through one of the holes. Wrap the other end with tape to make a "needle." Give the cards to the children and let them practice lacing the yarn in and out of the holes.

Variation: Instead of greeting cards, use old picture postcards or shapes cut from posterboard.

Gluing and Pasting

Provide the children with a variety of experiences that involve gluing or pasting small items. For example, let them glue or paste small squares of colored paper on pieces of construction paper to create mosaic designs. Or set out a box of scrap materials (fabric and paper pieces, small dried flowers, buttons, yarn, rickrack, sequins, etc.). Let the children glue or paste the materials on paper plates to make scrap collages. Or have the children make wood collages by gluing or pasting such items as twigs, wood shavings, toothpicks and Popsicle sticks on pieces of construction paper.

Hint: Use small jar lids for glue or paste containers. Provide cotton swabs for glue applicators and Popsicle sticks, small wooden spoons or strips of heavy cardboard for applying paste.

Taping

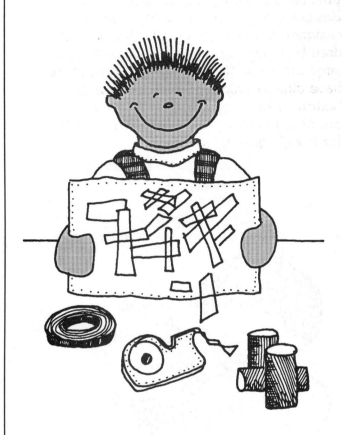

Let the children have fun working with different kinds of tape. Have them make collages by attaching short pieces of cellophane tape, colored plastic tape, adhesive tape, etc., to sheets of construction paper. Or provide them with rolls of masking tape and set out lightweight materials such as cardboard paper towel tubes, plastic foam food trays, egg cartons and small boxes. Let the children tear off pieces of the masking tape and use them to fasten the lightweight materials together any way they wish.

Buttons, Snaps and Zippers

Provide the children with opportunities to practice buttoning, snapping and zipping. Besides using commercial toys that are designed to teach these skills, let the children take turns dressing and undressing a large doll or stuffed animal with clothes that have different kinds of fasteners. Or cut button strips, snap strips and large zippers out of old clothing and place them in a box for the children to play with.

Connecting Dots

Draw dots at random on pieces of white construction paper. (Or use small circle stickers for dots.) Hand out the papers along with crayons or felt-tip markers. Let the children create designs on their papers by connecting the dots any way they wish.

Variation: Let the children work together to make a dot-to-dot mural. Hang a piece of butcher paper on a wall at the children's eye level. Give each child several circle stickers to use for dots. Have the children attach the stickers all over the butcher paper. Then let them draw lines from dot to dot with crayons to complete the mural.

Developing Holding Skills

Children need to develop holding and grasping skills before they are ready to write with pencils. To help them do this, provide them with a variety of experiences that involve grasping and manipulating different kinds of objects. Below are some suggestions.

- Picking up and playing with small toys.

- Playing with small objects in sand or water.

- Digging with small garden tools.

- Playing with and manipulating kitchen utensils.

- Measuring with small spoons.

- Cutting and spreading with dull knives.

- Stirring with large wooden spoons.

- Pounding and sawing with small carpentry tools.

- Brushing paint on paper with old toothbrushes.

- Dusting with feather dusters.

- Beating drums with drumsticks.

- Tapping out rhythms with rhythm sticks.

- Playing with hairbrushes and combs.

- Picking up and sorting such things as straws, Popsicle sticks and toy building logs.

Painting and Drawing

Before children can successfully learn to write, they need a lot of practice in making basic strokes. To help them develop skill in making circles that are round and closed and lines that are straight and smooth, create environments that invite the children to freely experiment with painting and drawing.

Painting — Give the children many opportunities to paint on large sheets of paper attached to walls or easels or placed on tables or on the floor. Provide the children with various kinds and sizes of brushes and let them experiment with using different kinds of paints such as watercolors, tempera paint and fingerpaint.

Drawing — Let the children use large crayons (with the paper wrappers removed) or large felt-tip markers to draw on a variety of kinds of paper such as construction paper, newsprint, butcher paper, plain wrapping paper and brown paper grocery bags. For a fun variation, give each child several different colored crayons that have been taped together and let the children enjoy making lines and circles in rainbow colors.

Drawing to Music

Use this activity to help the children develop fluid motions when making basic strokes. Hand out crayons and large sheets of paper. Then play an instrumental recording and let the children freely draw lines and circles to the music. Encourage them to draw as the music dictates. For example, they might make large round circles when the music is slow, short choppy marks when the music is fast, light curvy lines when the music is soft and strong bold lines when the music is loud. Continue the activity as long as interest lasts.

Dot-To-Dot Patterns

For a pre-writing activity that reinforces left-to-right progression, draw simple dot-to-dot patterns across pieces of paper as shown in the illustration. Begin each pattern with an extra-large dot to show where to begin and draw an arrow that points to the right to indicate direction. Give the papers to the children. Have them connect the dots with crayons or large pencils, encouraging them to make their lines as smooth and straight as possible.

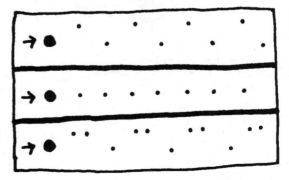

Follow the Lines

On a piece of 8½- by 11-inch paper, draw dots to create straight lines and wavy lines. Then make dotted-line outlines of several basic shapes such as a circle, a square and a triangle. Place the paper inside a clear plastic page protector. Let one child at a time trace over the dotted lines with a black crayon to create complete lines and shapes. After each child's turn, wipe the surface of the plastic page protector with a paper towel to remove the crayon marks.

Add-A-Stroke

On a separate piece of paper for each child, draw simple geometric shapes (a square, a circle, a triangle, etc.), leaving off one side of each shape. Give the papers to the children and let them complete the shapes by drawing lines with crayons or large pencils.

Erasable Paint Slate

Put a small amount of brightly colored fingerpaint into a quart-sized reclosable plastic freezer bag. Seal the bag and reinforce the edges with masking tape. Mount the bag on a larger piece of cardboard that has been covered with white self-stick paper. For extra security, place one-half of another freezer bag over the first bag and attach the edges to the cardboard. Let the children take turns using their fingers to draw lines and letters on the paint slate. Show them how to erase their drawings by smoothing over the slate with their hands.

Hint: While the children are drawing, remind them to rub with their fingertips, not scratch with their fingernails.

Chalkboard Writing

Place paintbrushes and a bucket of water beside a washable chalkboard. Print letters on the chalkboard with chalk. Let the children dip the paintbrushes into the water and trace over the chalk letters. Or let them use the wet brushes to create freehand letters on the chalkboard just after it has been erased.

Variation: Print letters on a small chalk slate and let the children trace over them with their fingers.

Writing in Sand

Provide the children with a sandbox. Show them how to smooth out the surface of the sand with their hands. Then let them take turns drawing letters in the sand with a finger, a Popsicle stick, a twig or a spoon.

Variation: Place about three inches of sand in a dishpan and add a little water. Let the children practice writing in the wet sand.

Writing in Snow

Just after a snowfall, help the children bundle up and take them outdoors. Look around for a patch of snow that is clear and unbroken. Give the children tongue depressors (or other kinds of safe sticks). Then let them have fun drawing lines or letters in the snow.

Variation: See the squeeze bottle activity on page 28.

Painting Letters

Talk about alphabet letters when the children are painting at easels. Point out how some shapes they have made look like certain letters. Then draw those letters on separate pieces of paper and have the children use brushes to paint over them.

Tracing Letters With Crayons

For each child print letters, short words or the child's name on a separate piece of lined writing paper. Cover the papers with clear self-stick paper. Let the children practice tracing over the letters or words on their papers with black crayons. When it's time to erase the crayon marks, wipe the surface of the papers with a tissue or a soft cloth.

Writing With Brushes and Water

Take the children outdoors on a sunny day. Give them each a small paintbrush and provide buckets of water. Let the children use the brushes and water to paint lines or letters on a fence, an outside wall, a sidewalk, a picnic table or any other appropriate surface.

Writing With Feathers

Give the children large sheets of construction paper. Set out different colors of tempera paint and long feathers. Let the children dip the feathers into the paint and use them like brushes to make basic strokes or letters on their papers.

Writing With Roll-On Bottles

Pry the roller tops off empty roll-on deodorant bottles. Wash the tops and the bottles thoroughly and allow them to dry. Then fill the bottles with different colors of liquid tempera paint and replace the roller tops. Let the children use the roll-on bottles to draw lines, shapes or letters on sheets of construction paper.

Writing With Squeeze Bottles

Collect plastic squeeze-type condiment bottles (the kind used for mustard and ketchup). Fill the bottles with different colors of extra-thick tempera paint. Let the children squeeze the paint onto large pieces of construction paper or butcher paper to create lines, shapes or letters.

Variation: Fill squeeze bottles with water and add drops of food coloring. Take the children outdoors and let them practice writing on sidewalks or snow with the colored water.

Salt Box

Cut black paper to fit inside the bottom of a sturdy shallow box and attach it in place. Cover the bottom of the box with a layer of salt. Let the children take turns drawing letters in the salt with their fingers. Show them how to erase their letters by gently shaking the box from side to side.

Erasable Tablet

Purchase an erasable tablet that comes with its own writing tool. (The tablets are available at variety and toy stores.) Let one child at a time practice drawing letters on the tablet. Show the child how to lift the sheet of plastic film on the tablet to erase his or her drawings.

Spaghetti Letters

Break dried spaghetti noodles in half and cook them according to the package directions. Drain the noodles and allow them to cool. Give each child a piece of waxed paper and some of the wet spaghetti. Let the children use the noodles to form different alphabet letters on their papers. If desired, conclude the activity by helping the children form the letters that spell their names. When the letters have dried, they can be glued on sheets of dark colored construction paper.

Variation: Let the children form spaghetti letters on squares of brightly colored posterboard. (The starch in the noodles will allow them to stick.)

Dough Letters

When the children are working with playdough, encourage them to try making letter shapes. Have them roll the dough into long snakes. Then show them how the snakes can be twisted and turned to form different letters. Follow the same procedure when the children are working with bread or pretzel dough. Then bake the letters according to the recipe directions.

Writing in Fingerpaint

While the children are fingerpainting, encourage them to try making different alphabet letters. If desired, use your finger to draw letters on the children's papers for them to trace over or copy. Have the children smooth out the paint when they are ready to try making new letters.

Writing in Shaving Cream

Spray puffs of shaving cream on cookie sheets, plain plastic trays or a washable tabletop. Let the children spread out the shaving cream with their hands and enjoy fingerpainting with it. Then show them how to use their pointer fingers to draw letters in the shaving cream.

Writing on Paper

For beginning writing activities, provide the children with big sheets of paper that can accommodate large-muscle controlled lines and squiggles. For example, give them paper grocery bags that have been cut open and laid out flat or pieces of butcher paper, wrapping paper or shelf paper. Check with local offices that do work on large paper, such as architectural, drafting or design offices. They often will give away used paper. Or ask offices that use computers to donate their discarded paper print-outs (children do not mind if there is printing on one side of their papers). Another source to check would be newspaper offices, which often have roll-ends of plain or colored newsprint that they will either give away or sell for a moderate fee.

Writing Tools – Let the children practice writing on paper with any of the materials listed below.

- Large crayons, with paper wrappers removed
- Large non-permanent felt-tip markers
- Large pieces of chalk
- Large pencils

Writing With Soap Crayons

Purchase boxes of soap crayons (available at many bath stores). Let the children use the crayons to write on the bottom and sides of a dry sink or bathtub or on any other similar surface. To erase the crayon marks, wipe them with a wet sponge or cloth.

Writing With Cotton Swabs

Cut egg cartons into thirds to make four-part paint containers. Pour small amounts of different colored tempera paint into the egg cups. Provide the children with cotton swabs and pieces of construction paper. Let them dip the swabs into the paint and use them like brushes to make lines, circles and letters on their papers.

Writing With Shoe Polish Bottles

Save empty white shoe polish bottles that have foam applicators attached to the tops. Pry off the tops and fill the bottles with different colors of diluted tempera paint. Let the children use the bottles like felt-tip markers to practice writing on sheets of construction paper.

Writing on Foil

For each child wrap a piece of heavy duty aluminum foil around a piece of smooth cardboard. Let the children practice writing on the foil with Popsicle sticks. To erase, have them smooth out the foil with their fingertips. When the activity is over, save the foil pieces to use for art projects.

Sidewalk Writing

When weather permits, take the children outdoors and let them write on a sidewalk or other paved surface with large pieces of chalk. To help develop large muscle coordination, have the children make basic strokes while moving their entire arms rather than just their hands and fingers. At the end of the activity, wash away the chalk marks with a garden hose.

Carbon Paper Writing

Assemble typing paper, carbon paper and paper clips. Make a "tablet" for each child by clipping together two sheets of typing paper with a piece of carbon paper in between. Place the tablets on a table, making sure that the shiny sides of the carbons are facing down. Let the children use large pencils to write letters on the top sheets of their tablets. Then have them lift their carbon papers to reveal the letter prints they have created on their bottom sheets. Use additional pieces of typing paper to make clean tablets as needed.

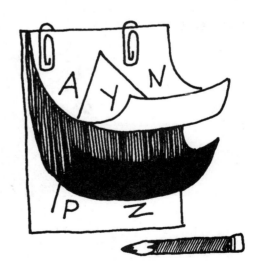

Writing With Glue

Have the children place pieces of construction paper inside large box lids. Give them small bottles of white liquid glue. Let them squeeze the glue onto their papers to create lines, shapes or letters. Then have them sprinkle sand or glitter on top of the glue and tap off the excess into the box lids.

Writing on Sandpaper

Cut large letter shapes out of sandpaper. Glue the letters on heavy cardboard squares. Then let the children take turns tracing over the sandpaper letters with pieces of chalk.

Writing Beginning Words

Follow the steps below when teaching a child how to write his or her name or any other beginning word.

Step One — Print the word near the top of a large piece of writing paper. Brush or squeeze glue over the letters and then sprinkle on sand. When the glue has dried, let the child practice tracing over the sand-covered word with his or her finger.

Step Two — Just below the sand lettering, print the same word again, this time using dotted lines. Cover the word with a strip of clear self-stick paper. Let the child print the word by tracing over the dotted-line letters with a black crayon. Then use a tissue or a paper towel to wipe off the crayon marks. Have the child repeat this step as many times as necessary.

Step Three — Give the child a separate piece of writing paper to place directly below the first piece. Then let the child try writing the word on his or her own. If the child has difficulty with the word, go back and repeat steps one and two before encouraging the child to try again.

Getting Ready to Read

- ◆ **Pre-Reading Concept Building Activities**
- ◆ **Pre-Reading Thinking Skill Activities**
- ◆ **Book Knowledge Activities**

Taped Sounds

Use a tape recorder to record familiar sounds (a telephone ringing, a vacuum cleaner buzzing, a clock ticking, a car starting, water splashing, etc.). Play the tape for the children and let them try to identify the different sounds.

Variation: Have the children take turns recording a sentence or two on tape. Later, let them listen to their recorded voices and try identifying the different speakers.

Matching Sounds

Collect two each of such objects as a bell, a ring of keys, a drum and a piece of paper. Place one set of the objects in front of a small partition and place the other set behind it. Sit behind the partition and make a sound with one of the objects. Ask a child to find the object in front of the partition that makes the same sound.

Variation: Fill pairs of small opaque plastic bottles with different materials such as dried beans, rice, salt and flour. Place the lids on the bottles and secure them with tape. Let the children take turns shaking the bottles to find those that make matching sounds.

High and Low

On a piano or a xylophone, play a full scale of notes up and down until the children become familiar with it. Then concentrate on the highest and lowest notes. Ask the children to reach their hands up high whenever they hear you play the high note and to place their hands down low whenever they hear you play the low note. If you think that your children can distinguish a middle-range note, have them fold their hands whenever they hear you play one. Continue as long as interest lasts.

Note: Keep in mind that the purpose of this activity is to teach sound discrimination, not music.

Following Directions

Help the children develop listening skills by giving them simple directions to follow. Start with one-step directions such as these: "Touch your ear; Touch your elbow; Take one step forward." Then gradually move on to two-step directions: "Touch your nose and then your knee; Take one step forward and one step backward." When the children have had lots of practice, let them try following three-step directions such as these: "Sit down, put your hands on your knees and wiggle your toes; Take one step forward, one step backward and clap your hands."

Variation: Play the game Simon Says.

Shape Board Game

Make a gameboard for each group of two or three children. In the upper left-hand corner of a large piece of construction paper, draw a circle and print "Start" inside of it. Then draw a pathway of geometric shapes (circles, squares, triangles, etc.), in random order, winding around the paper. End with a circle in the lower right-hand corner marked "Finish." Make three or four game cards for each shape by drawing the shapes on index cards. Put the deck of cards face down and give each child a different kind of game marker to place on the "Start" circle. As each child turns up a card, have the child move his or her marker to the next shape designated by the card. Have the children continue playing until everyone has reached the "Finish" circle. Then let them start the game again, if desired.

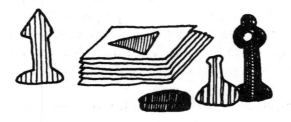

Shape Mailboxes

Make mailboxes by covering the lids of three or more shoeboxes with construction paper and cutting a slit in the top of each lid. Put the lids on the boxes. On an index card for each mailbox draw a different shape (a circle, a triangle, a star, etc.). Tape the cards to the backs of the mailboxes so that they stand above the lids. Make three or four "letters" for each mailbox by drawing matching shapes on the fronts of sealed envelopes. Then mix up the envelopes and let the children take turns mailing them through the slots in the appropriate mailboxes.

Shape Cubes

Select two or three clear plastic photo cubes and cut index cards to fit in the sides. Put cards on which you have drawn different basic shapes (a circle, a square, a diamond, a heart, etc.) into the sides of one cube. Then put cards on which you have drawn matching shapes into the sides of the other cube or cubes. Set out the cubes and let the children move them around to find the shapes that are alike.

Shape Books

Make a book for each child by stapling pieces of white paper together with a construction paper cover. Print "My Shape Book" and the child's name on the front. Label the pages of the book with drawings of a circle, a square, a triangle and a rectangle. Set out precut magazine pictures of objects that are round, square, triangular and rectangular. Help the children identify the shapes on the pages of their books. Then let them choose the matching shaped pictures they want and glue them on the appropriate pages.

Variation: Let the children make separate books for each shape.

Shape Card Game

Select twelve index cards and divide them into three sets of four cards each. Using a felt-tip marker, draw triangles on one set of cards, circles on another set and squares on the remaining set. To play, lay out three cards containing matching shapes and one card containing a shape that is different. Then ask the children to identify the different shape and to tell why it doesn't belong with the other three. Continue the game, using other combinations of cards.

Variation: Make four cards containing pictures of triangular objects (a clown hat, a tepee, etc.), four cards containing pictures of circular objects (a ball, a clock face, etc.) and four cards containing pictures of square objects (a box, an alphabet block, etc.).

Shape Puzzle Board

Make a gameboard by tracing around several different shaped objects (a key, a cookie cutter, a tongue depressor, a jar lid, etc.) on a piece of posterboard. Cover the gameboard with clear self-stick paper, if desired. Set out the gameboard along with the objects. Let the children take turns placing the objects on the matching shaped tracings on the gameboard.

Shape Lotto Game

Make a gameboard by dividing a 9-inch square of posterboard into nine squares. In each square draw a different shape (a circle, a triangle, a heart, a star, etc.). Make game cards by drawing matching shapes on nine 3-inch squares cut from posterboard. To play, let the children take turns placing the game cards on top of the matching squares on the gameboard.

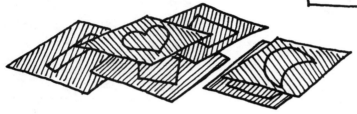

Shape Folder

On the insides of a file folder draw eight basic shapes (a circle, a square, a diamond, a heart, etc.). Draw matching shapes on posterboard and cut them out. If desired, cover the file folder and the cutouts with clear self-stick paper. Then lay the open file folder on a table and put the cutouts in a pile. Let the children take turns placing the cutouts on top of the matching shapes on the file folder.

Shape Sticks

Turn a shoebox upside down and cut two parallel rows of five slits each in the top. At the tops of five tongue depressors, attach stickers cut into different basic shapes (a circle, a triangle, a star, a heart, etc.). Attach matching shaped stickers to the tops of five more tongue depressors. Insert one set of tongue depressors in one of the rows of slits in the shoebox. Then let the children take turns inserting matching tongue depressors from the second set in the appropriate slits in the other row.

Shape Puzzles

Cut four or five large index cards into two-part puzzles. Draw a different basic shape (a circle, a square, a triangle, etc.) on one part of each puzzle and a matching shape on the other part. Then mix up the puzzle pieces and let the children take turns finding the match-ups.

Concentration

Select eight small index cards and divide them into pairs. On each pair draw a different shape (a triangle, a heart, a star, etc.). Mix up the cards and spread them out face down on a table or on the floor. Let one child begin by turning up two cards. If the shapes match, let the child keep the cards. If the shapes don't match, have the child replace both cards face down exactly where they were before. Continue the game until all the cards have been matched. Then let the child who ended up with the most cards have the first turn when you start the game again.

Variation: Attach different pairs of matching picture stickers to the cards. Or glue on small matching pictures cut from different kinds of wrapping paper.

Picture Matching Game

On each of ten index cards draw an identical heart shape (or any other shape desired). Divide the cards into pairs. Color or decorate the hearts on each pair of cards differently. Then mix up the cards and let the children take turns finding the matching pairs of hearts.

Variation: Use this activity for matching such things as jack-o'-lantern faces, Easter eggs or decorated Christmas trees. Or draw a different animal, fruit, vegetable, etc., on each pair of cards.

Poker Chip Patterns

Collect a number of red and white poker chips and place them in a box. Invite a child to sit with you while you line up several chips in a color pattern such as red, white, red, white. Ask the child to use chips from the box to continue the pattern. Then start a more complicated pattern for the child to continue, such as red, white, white, red, white, white. When the child has become familiar with the game, take turns creating beginning patterns with him or her. If you have enough poker chips, let several children at a time have fun repeating and creating color patterns.

Variation: Instead of poker chips, use such objects as different colored buttons or different geometric shapes cut from felt.

Table Settings

On the snack table make a simple place setting using a placemat, a plate, a cup, a napkin, a knife, a fork and a spoon. Talk with the children about the arrangement of the different objects. Then let them use the setting as a guide to create additional place settings on the table for lunch or snacktime.

Popsicle Stick Shapes

Invite several children at a time to sit with you on the floor. Set out a pile of Popsicle sticks. Arrange a few of the sticks on the floor in a simple shape such as a triangle. Then let the children use additional sticks to try copying the shape. Continue the game by making other shapes such as a square, a rectangle, a diamond or a house.

Toothpick Patterns

Sit with one or two children at a table. Line up several toothpicks in a simple pattern (two vertical, one horizontal, two vertical, one horizontal, etc.). Then give the children some toothpicks and let them try duplicating the pattern. Continue in the same manner, each time making your pattern more complicated.

Variation: Draw patterns of lines on large index cards. Let the children select cards and duplicate the patterns with toothpicks.

Feelie Box

Cut the bottom out of a round oatmeal box. Find an old pair of large socks and cut off the feet. Slip the sock tops over the ends of the box and secure them with tape. Then cover the box with colored or patterned self-stick paper. Place a small toy or other object inside the box. Let a child put one or both hands in the ends of the socks, reach into the box and try to identify the object inside by feeling it.

Variation: Use a small coffee can instead of an oatmeal box. Smooth over any sharp edges after removing the top and the bottom of the can.

Texture Match

Cut eight to ten 3-inch squares out of cardboard. Cover each pair of squares with a different kind of textured material (sandpaper, flocked wallpaper, aluminum foil, felt, corduroy, etc.). Place one of each pair in a bag and set the rest out on a table. Let the children take turns choosing a square from the table and then reaching into the bag to find its match by touch.

Variation: Place three or four sets of matching squares on a table. Have the children take turns closing their eyes and moving their hands over the squares to find the match-ups.

Matching Scents

Collect six small plastic bottles and place a cotton ball inside each one. Divide the bottles into pairs. In each pair place drops of a different scent (cologne, lemon juice, onion juice, peppermint food flavoring, etc.). If desired, cover the bottles with aluminum foil and punch small holes in the tops. Let the children take turns sniffing the bottles and trying to match the scents that are alike.

Taste and Tell

At snacktime have the children close their eyes while you give them each an orange segment or other small item of food. With their eyes still closed, have the children take small bites of the item. Can they tell by the taste what food they are eating? Continue in the same manner, each time giving the children a different food item to taste (a pickle, a small piece of cheese, a cracker, a banana slice, etc.).

Sorting Shapes

From red posterboard cut out a large circle, a medium-sized square and a small triangle. From blue posterboard cut out a large square, a medium-sized triangle and a small circle. From yellow posterboard cut out a large triangle, a medium-sized circle and a small square. Mix up the shapes and lay them out on a table or on the floor. Let the children take turns sorting the shapes into piles by color, by size and then by shape.

Sorting Buttons

Set out a basket containing a large assortment of buttons. Provide the children with muffin tins or similar kinds of containers. Then let the children practice sorting the buttons by color, by size, by shape, by number of holes and by kind of material (plastic, fabric, metal, etc.).

Sorting Shells

Put together a collection of different kinds of shells (available at import shops and craft stores). Have the children sit with you in a circle. Pass around the shells for the children to touch and examine. Talk with them about the different sizes, textures, shapes and colors of the shells. Then let the children sort the shells into groups according to size (large and small), texture (rough and smooth), shape or color.

Mix and Sort

Collect a number of red, yellow and blue crayons, blocks and wooden beads. Place the objects in a shallow box and mix them up. Set out three empty baskets or similar containers. Let the children take turns sorting the objects into the three baskets first by color, then by kind.

Variation: Use any three combinations of objects (toy cars, plastic clothespins, colored rubber bands, etc.) and any three combinations of colors.

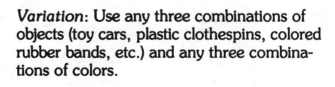

All Around the House

Divide a piece of butcher paper into four sections to represent rooms in a house. Label the sections to indicate a living room, a bedroom, a bathroom and a kitchen. Cut out magazine pictures of various objects that would be found in each of the four rooms. Cover the pictures with clear self-stick paper, if desired. Then let the children take turns placing the pictures in the appropriate rooms on the butcher paper.

Variation: Adapt the game to use for classifying such things as animals (zoo animals, farm animals, sea animals, pets) or plants (trees, flowers, vegetables, fruits).

Which One Doesn't Belong?

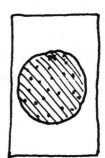

Select four large index cards. On three of the cards draw pictures of things that are alike in some way, such as an apple, an orange and a banana. On the fourth card draw a picture of something that is unlike the other three, such as a clock. Follow the same procedure to make other sets of four cards each. To play, spread out a set of cards on a table or on the floor. Invite a child to look at the pictures and tell you which one doesn't belong. Encourage the child to try explaining his or her answer. Continue in the same manner, using the other sets of cards.

Hard and Soft Box

In a box place a variety of items that are hard (blocks, crayons, spools, rocks, keys, etc.) and a variety of items that are soft (cotton balls, fabric pieces, rubber bands, modeling clay, socks, etc.). Let the children take turns emptying the box onto the floor and placing the hard items in one pile and the soft items in another pile.

Clothes for the Family

Bring in a large basket containing items of clothing for a family. Include clothes for a father, a mother, a boy, a girl and a baby. Let several children at a time work together to sort the clothes into piles for the different family members. If the clothes include an item that might be worn by more than one family member, let the children decide in which pile to place it. Have the children mix up the clothes and put them back into the basket when their turns are over.

Sequence Cards

Draw pictures on index cards that illustrate a sequence of events. For example, to show the stages of a bird hatching, draw pictures of the egg in its nest, the egg cracking, the bird partly out of the shell and the bird completely hatched. Or to show the growth stages of a flower, draw pictures of a seed in the ground, the seed sprouting, the flower in bud and the flower in bloom. Mix up the cards and spread them out on a table. Let the children take turns arranging the cards in the proper sequence.

Picture Sequence Charts

Make picture charts for the children to refer to when they are doing activities that involve sequential steps. For example, if you wish to have the children make their own pudding to use for fingerpainting, create a picture chart like the one shown in the illustration. The chart explains these four steps: Place 2 teaspoons instant pudding plus 4 teaspoons milk in a baby food jar; Put on the lid and shake the jar well; Pour the pudding on a piece of paper; Paint designs in the pudding with hands. After providing the children with the necessary utensils and ingredients for the activity, read through the chart several times. Then let the children try following the illustrated steps on their own.

Comic Strip Sequencing

Cut appropriate comic strips out of newspapers. Read and discuss the strips with the children. Then cut each strip into panels and place them in separate piles. Let the children take turns putting the panels back in the proper order.

Picture Book Sequencing

Purchase two copies of a small inexpensive picture book that tells a simple story. Cut the pictures out of one of the copies, mix them up and set them aside. Use the other copy of the book to read the story to the children. After each reading, place the cutout pictures on a table or on the floor. Let the children put the pictures together in the proper sequence.

Photo Recall

Use an instant camera to take snapshots of the children as they are working in different learning areas. Later, show the pictures to the children. Encourage them to recall what they were doing in each area when the photos were taken.

Variation: Take photographs during a field trip or on some other special occasion. At a later date, show the pictures to the children and let them recall their experiences.

Storytime Recall

At storytime reread or retell favorite stories. As you do so, pause occasionally to let the children fill in familiar words or tell what happens next. Or show just the pictures from a familiar storybook and ask the children to tell what is happening in each one.

What's Missing?

Have the children sit with you in a circle. In the middle place five or six items (small toys, Christmas decorations, nature items, etc.). Name each of the items with the group. Then have the children close their eyes while you remove one of the items. When the children open their eyes, have them try to guess what's missing.

Variation: For a more challenging game, move the items around before the children open their eyes.

End-Of-Day Recall

Just before the children go home, let them take turns acting out a favorite activity they did that day. Have the others try guessing what the activity was. Or ask the children to recall such things as the day's snack or a new song they learned to sing.

Fun With Rhymes

Listening to simple verses and anticipating rhyming words that fit the context helps children to develop thinking skills. Select appropriate nursery rhymes like the ones that follow. Read them aloud and let the children fill in the blanks.

Mary Had a Little Lamb

Mary had a little lamb,
Its fleece was white as snow.
And everywhere that Mary went
The lamb was sure to _____.

It followed her to school one day,
Which was against the rule.
It made the children laugh and play
To see a lamb at _____.

Traditional

Rain on the Green Grass

Rain on the green grass,
Rain on the tree,
Rain on the housetop,
But not on _____.

Traditional

There Was an Old Woman

There was an old woman
Who lived on a hill,
And if she's not gone
She lives there _____.

Traditional

More Fun With Rhymes

Recite teaching rhymes like the ones on this page and let the children supply the rhyming words.

Six Buzzing Bumblebees

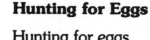

Six buzzing bumblebees
Flying around the hive,
One buzzes off
And that leaves _____.

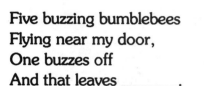

Five buzzing bumblebees
Flying near my door,
One buzzes off
And that leaves _____.

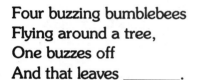

Four buzzing bumblebees
Flying around a tree,
One buzzes off
And that leaves _____.

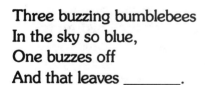

Three buzzing bumblebees
In the sky so blue,
One buzzes off
And that leaves _____.

Two buzzing bumblebees
Flying by the sun,
One buzzes off
And that leaves _____.

One buzzing bumblebee
Looking for some fun,
It buzzes off
And that leaves _____.

Susan M. Paprocki

Hunting for Eggs

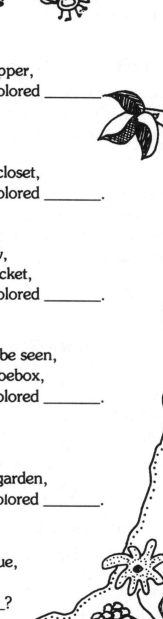

Hunting for eggs,
Under my bed,
I found one in a slipper,
And the egg was colored _____.

Hunting for eggs,
Now I have two,
I found one in the closet,
And the egg was colored _____.

Hunting for eggs,
What a lucky fellow,
I found one in a bucket,
And the egg was colored _____.

Hunting for eggs,
Where none could be seen,
I found one in a shoebox,
And the egg was colored _____.

Hunting for eggs,
Quick as a wink,
I found one in the garden,
And the egg was colored _____.

Red and yellow,
Green, pink and blue,
I found five eggs,
How about _____?

Jean Warren

From Here to There

Draw a map of a play town on a large piece of paper. Include intersecting roads, a park, several houses, a grocery store, a gas station, etc. Tape the map to the floor and provide the children with toy cars. Let several children at a time start their cars at the same place on the map and find different ways to drive to the same destination.

Variation: Draw a simple map on a piece of posterboard and cover it with clear self-stick paper. Let the children use their fingers to trace routes on the map.

How Could You Use It?

Give each child a large scarf or a square of lightweight fabric. Then ask the children to come up with as many different ways to use their scarves as they can. For example, they might wear them as capes or skirts, use them for doll blankets or for carrying small objects, fold them to create different shapes, fly them like flags, or tie them together to make a long "rope."

Variation: Follow the same procedure using other objects such as cardboard tubes, plastic foam food trays or paper bags.

I Wonder Why

Look through magazines to find unusual pictures that invite speculation about what might be happening (a dog sitting in a baby carriage, a man walking down the street with towel over his head, etc.). At circle time choose one of the pictures to show to the children. Ask them to think of as many reasons as they can to explain what is happening in the picture. Encourage them to use their imaginations, reminding them that there are no right or wrong answers.

What If?

Ask the children a "what-if?" question such as "What if you were no bigger than your thumb?" Encourage the children to respond freely. Then expand the discussion by asking more specific questions. For example: "If you were no bigger than your thumb, where would you sleep? What would you use for a bathtub? How would you lift a pencil? How would you write with it?" Below are more examples of "what-if?" questions.

- What if your pet could talk?
- What if you had wings?
- What if houses were made of gingerbread?
- What if you had your own robot?
- What if it rained all the time?

Holiday Problems

Make up holiday problems like the ones below for the children to try solving. Encourage them to use their imaginations when thinking up solutions.

Halloween — Some children want to make a jack-o'-lantern for Halloween but no pumpkins are available. What can they do? (They can use an orange to make a jack-o'-lantern; They can paint a round stone orange and add black facial features; They can cut a face out of an orange sack and put a candle inside; etc.).

Christmas — Santa's reindeer have all caught colds and won't be able to pull his sleigh on Christmas Eve. How can Santa deliver his presents to the children? (He can use an airplane to pull his sleigh; He can fly in a helicopter; He can send the presents by mail; etc.).

Easter — The Easter Bunny is coloring his eggs but he has run out of egg dye. How else can he decorate his eggs? (He can color them with paint or crayons; He can attach colorful stickers; He can glue on yarn, sequins or glitter; etc.).

Ice Cream Flavors

Ask the children to pretend that they have just opened an ice cream store. Then have them use their imaginations to think up some special ice cream flavors. For example, what about watermelon ice cream? Grape ice cream? Peanut butter and jelly ice cream? Spaghetti ice cream? Encourage the children to name as many flavors as they can, reminding them that there are no right or wrong answers.

How Many Ways?

Ask questions like the ones below and let the children act out or tell their responses.

- How many ways can you cross the room?
- How many ways can you play with a ball?
- How many way can you sing a song?
- How many ways can you eat peanut butter?
- How many ways can you show you are happy?
- How many way can you crack open a nut?
- How many way can you keep cool in summertme?

Silly Sentences

Have the children sit with you in a circle. Make up silly factual sentences such as these: "The sun froze my milk this morning; I saw some fish swimming in the sky; The rain dried up the flowers in the garden." Ask the children to tell what is wrong with your sentences. Then encourage them to make up similar silly sentences of their own.

What Happened Before?

Show the children a picture that clearly suggest some previous action. An example would be a picture of a child drying off a wet dog with a towel. Ask the children to make up sentences telling what might have happened before the picture was taken. Some possible responses: "The dog just had a bath; The dog ran through the sprinkler; The dog went swimming in a pool; The dog was out in the rain." Follow the same procedure using other similar pictures.

Picture Cube Roll

Fill the sides of a clear plastic photo cube with pictures of familiar items (a teddy bear, a pumpkin, a truck, a baby, etc.). Let one child at a time roll the cube like a die and name the pictured item that comes up. Then ask the child to tell a sentence or two about the item.

Variation: Give older children two picture cubes to roll. Let them make up sentences that include both of the pictured items that come up.

Silly Stories

On separate index cards draw or glue pictures of familiar objects (a tree, a pumpkin, a pizza, a house, a wagon, etc.). Place the cards in a bag and have the children sit with you in a circle. Let one child begin by removing two cards from the bag and holding them up. As the child does so, ask: "How did the (name of first pictured object) get in/on the (name of second pictured object)?" For example, if the child holds up pictures of a pizza and a tree, ask: "How did the pizza get in the tree?" Let the children have fun thinking up possible answers to the question. Encourage them to use their imaginations and to express their ideas in complete sentences. Continue until each child has had a turn choosing cards from the bag.

Parts of a Book

Invite one child at a time to sit with you while you read aloud a familiar storybook. When you have finished, give the closed book to the child. Ask him or her to show you the front of the book. The top of the book. The back of the book. Talk about the book covers and the spine. Then ask the child to open the book and find the beginning of the story, the end of the story, the top of a page, a word in the book, a picture in the book, etc.

Book Titles and Authors

Show the children several familiar storybooks. Help them to see that all the books have titles which appear on the front covers. Discuss how the titles help readers know what the books are about. Then talk about how the books are written by authors. Point out that the authors' names appear on the front covers of the books also.

Extension: Give the children opportunities to become authors by letting them create their own simple books (color books, number books, animal books, etc.). Provide them with blank books made by stapling sheets of white paper together with colored construction paper covers. Have the children glue appropriate magazine pictures on their book pages. Then help them write their titles and names on the front covers

Handling Books

Children learn respect for books by observing how adults handle them. Show that you value books by treating them with care and storing them in bookshelves or other appropriate places. Help the children learn proper ways to hold books and turn the pages. Whenever you introduce a newly purchased book, demonstrate how to gently open it and smooth out the pages before reading it. Throughout the day remind the children to carefully replace their books in the library corner when they have finished reading them.

From Left to Right

When reading a book to a child, help him or her understand that words on a page are written from left to right. Place the child's index finger on the beginning word of the story. Then gently move the child's finger across the page as you read the first sentence. Continue in the same manner while reading the rest of the story.

Variation: To provide practice in left-to-right progression, give each child a paper with lines of arrows and picture stickers on it as shown in the illustration. Have the child start at the largest sticker and move a finger across the paper to the other stickers in the direction indicated by the arrows. As he or she does so, have the child name the stickers or make up a simple story about them.

Parts of a Story

Talk with the children about how stories in books have a beginning, a middle and an end. For example, in "The Three Bears" the beginning of the story tells how Goldilocks visits the bears' empty house; the middle of the story tells how Goldilocks tastes the porridge, sits in the chairs and tries out the beds; and the end of the story tells how Goldilocks runs away after the bears come home and find her asleep. Read a short familiar storybook to the children. When you have finished, ask them to recall what happened at the beginning of the story, in the middle of the story and at the end.

Book Illustrations and Text

When reading a storybook to the children, explain that the pictures are called illustrations. Point out that the printed text tells the story in words and sentences and that the illustrations help to tell the story. As you read different pages of the text, ask the children to point to parts of the illustrations that show what the words and sentences are describing.

Developing a Love of Books

Instilling a love of books in children is one of the most important things adults can do. Following are just a few suggestions for helping your children grasp the idea that pleasure and information can come from words written on paper:

• Set aside special times each day to read to the children.

• Expose the children to a wide variety of books.

• Provide a reading corner that invites children to explore books on their own.

• Take the children on regular visits to the library.

• Show the children how answers to questions they ask can often be found in books.

• Demonstrate how you use such books as dictionaries, encyclopedias, craft books and cookbooks.

Keep in mind that children model what they see others doing. If you read and enjoy books, so will your children.

Vocabulary
Building

◆ **Vocabulary Building Activities**

Show and Tell

The traditional Show and Tell activity provides one of the best opportunities for helping young children develop vocabulary skills. Schedule regular times for Show and Tell throughout the week. Let the children who wish to participate take turns sharing items they have made or brought from home. Ask questions about the shared items that encourage the children to use descriptive words.

Note: Make sure that no child is forced to take part in the activity if he or she is reluctant to do so.

Room Conversations

As the children are playing, walk around the room and encourage them to tell you what they are doing. Ask them to describe such things as block structures, paintings, clay figures or dress-up costumes. If desired, carry a tablet and a pencil with you and have the children dictate short stories about what they are doing. Arrange a time later for sharing the stories with the entire group.

Category Game

At circle time choose a category such as Animals. Then let the children take turns naming as many different kinds of animals as they can. If necessary, help generate ideas by showing pictures of animals or by asking such questions as these: "Can you think of any animals that live on the farm? In the zoo? In the ocean?" When the children become familiar with the game, let them help choose the categories (Foods, Toys, Things Found in a House, Christmas Things, etc.).

Group Picture Game

Bring in interesting photographs or pictures cut from magazines. Sit with several children at a time and invite them to make simple statements about what they see in the pictures. Encourage them to speculate about what might have happened before or after the pictures were taken.

Variation: Set out magazines and let the children find their own picture to share and discuss.

What Did I See?

Read aloud a verse of the poem below. Then repeat the verse and let the children take turns filling in the blank. Continue in the same manner with the other verses.

I looked outside and what did I see?
A beautiful _____ smiling at me.

I looked up high and what did I see?
A colorful _____ smiling at me.

I looked in a box and what did I see?
A teeny tiny _____ smiling at me.

Jean Warren

Waiter, Waiter

Ask the children to name some of their favorite foods. Then recite the poem below and let them take turns filling in the blanks.

Waiter, waiter on the run,
I love _____,
Bring me one.

Waiter, waiter dressed in blue,
I love _____,
Bring me two.

Waiter, waiter by the tree,
I love _____,
Bring me three.

Waiter, waiter by the door,
I love _____,
Bring me four.

Waiter, waiter, sakes alive,
I love _____,
Bring me five.

Jean Warren

Stop and Shop

Let the children take turns filling in the blanks as you recite the "Stop and Shop" poem below. Shop suggestions include a toy shop, a grocery shop, a pet shop, a hardware shop, a clothing shop, a car shop and a bakery shop. Continue the poem by adding verses about the second stop, the third stop, and so on.

The first stop's a _____ shop.
What will I buy today?
A _____ for me,
A _____ for Mother,
A _____ for Sister
And a _____ for Brother.
That's what I'll buy today.

Jean Warren

Zoo Animals

Let the children take turns naming zoo animals. After each child's turn have the children sing the song below, filling in the blank with the animal's name.

Sung to: "Have You Ever Seen a Lassie?"

Have you ever seen the _____,
The _____, the _____?
Have you ever seen the _____
That lives in the zoo?
That lives in the zoo,
That lives in the zoo.
Have you ever seen the _____,
That lives in the zoo?

Jean Warren

Learning Rhymes

Provide as many opportunities as possible for the children to learn and recite nursery rhymes. Below are two favorites to get you started. You might also wish to check your local library for sources of other simple poems and rhymes that are appropriate for teaching to young children.

Jack Be Nimble

Jack be nimble,
Jack be quick,
Jack jump over
The candlestick.

Traditional

Mistress Mary

Mistress Mary, quite contrary,
How does your garden grow?
With silver bells and cockle shells,
And pretty maids all in a row.

Traditional

Rhyming Games

- Ask a child to say a word. Then you name a rhyming word.

- Say a simple word like "cat." Ask a child to name a rhyming word.

- Make a deck of cards on which you have drawn pictures of such things as a hat, a pan, a ball and a tree. Let the children take turns choosing a card, naming the picture on it and then saying a rhyming word.

Activity Time Extensions

Take advantage of different activity times to help the children increase their vocabulary skills. Below are a few suggestions.

Art Time — Ask the children to describe the different colors, shapes and lines in their artwork. Encourage them also to express how different pictures or colors make them feel.

Science Time — When the children are observing and discussing a nature item, help them to learn the names of its parts (a fish has scales, fins, gills, etc.). Also, help them to express new descriptive words when they are experimenting with different substances or objects (ice is transparent; mirrors reflect images; etc.).

Storytime — When you finish reading a book to the children, extend the story by asking questions. For example, if the book is about a pumpkin you might ask: "What are some words that remind you of a pumpkin? If you wanted to grow a pumpkin, what would you need? What are some things you could do with a pumpkin?"

Snacktime — While the children are enjoying their snack, ask them to describe the different tastes and textures of the foods they are eating. Encourage them to use such words as these: "sweet, salty, hard, soft, creamy, crunchy."

Find It and Name It

Throughout the day encourage the children to find and name objects that are pictured on charts, posters or in books. Or play a simple riddle game at circle time. Start by saying to a child, "I'm thinking of something that is (red, round and that bounces)." Then have the child search for the object, bring it back to the circle and name it (a ball). Continue until everyone has had a turn. When the children become familiar with the game, let them take turns giving the clues, if desired.

I Wish

Play wishing games with the children at circle time. Start by saying something like, "I wish I could have pizza for dinner tonight." Then let each child in turn repeat the sentence, substituting the name of a different food for the word "pizza." Continue with other sentences such as these: "I wish I could take a ride in a _____; I wish I could have a _____ for a pet; I wish I could go to a toy store and buy a _____."

Picture Stories

Provide the children with many opportunities to read wordless picture books. Encourage them to express what the pictures tell them. Or set out interesting pictures that have been cut from magazines. Let each child have a turn choosing a picture and telling a story about it.

Sack Stories

For each child place a small toy or other object in a paper sack. (If desired, use objects that relate to a particular topic such as the circus or St. Patrick's Day.) Start telling a simple story. Then let the children take turns choosing objects from the sack and holding them up. As they do so, incorporate the objects into your story. Continue until all the objects have been used.

Variation: If you work with older children, let them make up their own sentences about the objects they take from the sack.

Alphabet Letters

◆ **Letter Shape Activities**
◆ **Letter Recognition Activities**

Textured Letters

Cut alphabet letters out of a textured material such as sandpaper, felt or flocked wallpaper. Glue the letters on separate cardboard squares. Let the children trace over the letters with their fingers or hands. Have them try it first with their eyes open, then with their eyes closed.

Tracing Letters With Fingers

Let the children use their fingers to trace over letters that have been drawn with chalk on a chalkboard or made with pieces of masking tape on a wall. Or provide the children with letter stencils to trace over with their fingers.

Flashlight Writing

Print extra-large letters on a chalkboard or on pieces of butcher paper attached to a wall. Turn on flashlights, give them to the children and darken the room. Let the children trace over the letters on the chalkboard or wall with the beams of their flashlights.

Writing in Air

Let the children practice drawing giant alphabet letters in the air with their arms. If necessary, display letters for them to copy, or guide the children as they are drawing. When the children become familiar with the activity, let them try writing their names or simple words in the air.

Net Letter Holder

Staple nylon netting to a large index card along the two long edges, leaving the sides open. Print alphabet letters on slightly smaller cards. Slip one card at a time under the netting. Let the children take turns tracing the letter over the netting with a finger while saying the letter's name.

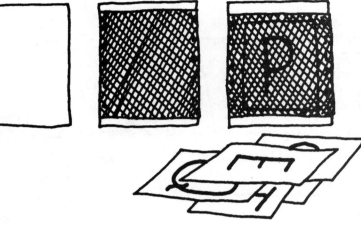

Tracing Letters on Backs

Invite one child at a time to play this simple game with you. Use a finger to trace alphabet letters on the child's back and have him or her try guessing what letters you are drawing. Then let the child trace letters on your back for you to guess. Continue playing the game until each child has had a turn.

Floor Letters

Make large alphabet letters on the floor with pieces of masking tape. Let the children take turns walking, skipping or crawling on the tape letters. Or have the children place blocks or other objects on the tape to create large three-dimensional letters.

Variation: On a carpeted floor form alphabet letters with textured materials such as cotton balls, pieces of yarn or strips of fabric. Encourage the children to lightly trace over the letters with their hands.

Body Letters

Encourage the children to use their fingers, hands and whole bodies to form alphabet letters. For example, show them how to form such letters as *C, P* or *O* with their hands and fingers. Or have them stand and use their whole bodies to form such letters as *I, T* or *Y*. If desired, let pairs of children try working together to form different letters.

Extension: Have groups of children lie on the floor and use their bodies to form such letters as *A, W* or *H*.

Painting on Letter Shapes

Cut large letter shapes out of construction paper or butcher paper. Have the children paint the letters with seasonal colors, encouraging them to brush on the paint as the letters are written. If desired, let the children sprinkle salt or glitter on the wet paint to add texture.

Variation: Instead of using paint, let the children color the letter shapes with crayons or felt-tip markers.

Lacing Letter Shapes

Draw large letter shapes on posterboard or other heavy paper. Help the children cut out the shapes with scissors. Then let them take turns using a hole punch to punch holes around the edges of their letters. For each child cut off a long piece of yarn. Tie one end through a hole in his or her letter shape and wrap tape around the other end to make a "needle." Show the children how to lace their yarn pieces in and out of the holes around their letters. When the children have finished, trim the loose yarn ends and tape them to the backs of the letter shapes.

Thumbprint Letters

For each child print large alphabet letters (or the child's name) on a separate piece of paper. Set out commercial ink pads and give the children their papers. Show the children how to press their thumbs on the inkpads. Then have them trace over the letters on their papers by stamping on their thumbprints.

Nail Letters

Collect large blocks of softwood. Print an alphabet letter on each block with a felt-tip marker. Place the wood blocks in a supervised carpentry area and let the children outline the letters with nails or screws.

Variation: Print letters on large blocks of plastic foam and let the children outline them with golf tees.

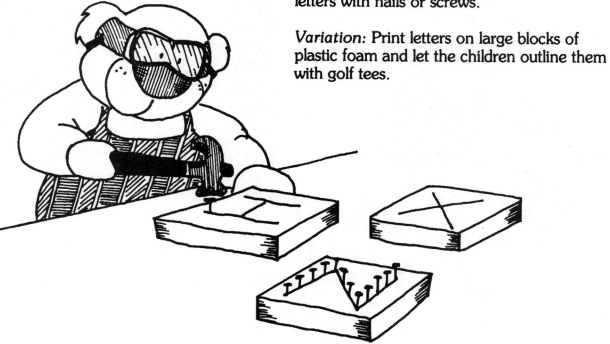

Letters Everywhere

Whenever you introduce a new alphabet letter, help the children discover that letter in different places around the room (on posters, charts, book covers, etc.). Or take the children on a neighborhood walk and have them look for the letter in signs they see along the way.

Extension: For a simple game, let the children try to find the alphabet letter on empty cereal boxes, soup cans and other food containers that have been placed on a table or on the floor.

Letter Detective

Choose an alphabet letter such as *B*. Print *B*'s and other letters on separate Post-it brand notes and stick the notes around the room where the children can find them easily. Select one child to be the Letter Detective and give him or her a magnifying glass. Have the Letter Detective walk around the room and search for "evidence of *B*." When the child finds a *B* note, have him or her bring it back to you. Then choose another child to be the Letter Detective. Continue until all the *B* notes have been found. Adapt the game to review any alphabet letter desired.

Show You Know

Have the children perform actions to show that they recognize alphabet letters. For example, choose a letter such as *H*. Print *H*'s on five or six index cards and print other letters on several more cards. Ask the children to stand in front of you. Then hold up the cards, one at a time, and have the children hop each time they see the letter *H*.

Variation: Have the children bow for *B*, clap for *C*, jump for *J*, smile for *S*, wave for *W*, etc.

Newspaper Letters

Give the children newspaper sections and felt-tip markers. Have each child look for the letter his or her first name begins with and circle it. Or choose a letter you wish to review and have the children circle that letter.

Variation: Help the children cut out the letters they find. Then let them glue their letters on pieces of construction paper to make collages.

Musical Letters

Select a letter you have been working on such as *A*. Print *A*'s and other letters on separate pieces of construction paper and tape the papers to the floor. Then play music and have the children walk around the room. Whenever you stop the music, have each child find an *A* to stand on. Continue the game as long as interest lasts.

Letter Puppets

Choose an alphabet letter such as *D*. Give each child a Popsicle stick, a dried pasta *D* shape and a small picture or cutout of something whose name begins with *D* (a dinosaur, a dog, a doll, etc.). Have the children glue their pictures on the top parts of their Popsicle sticks and their pasta letters on the center parts. When the glue has dried, let the children use their puppets while telling stories or singing songs.

Variation: Use cereal alphabet letters and tongue depressors instead of pasta letters and Popsicle sticks.

Alphabet Scrapbook

Make a blank book by putting 26 large pieces of white paper together with a colored paper cover. Punch holes on the left-hand side and insert metal rings. Label the pages from *A* to *Z*. Choose one page at a time and review the letter on it with the children. Help them to cut examples of the letter from newspaper headlines, magazine article titles or catalog ads. Also provide several pictures of things whose names begin with the letter. Then let the children glue the letters and pictures on the book page any way they wish. When your alphabet scrapbook is complete, place it in the library corner for the children to enjoy "reading."

Alphabet Take-Home Items

Whenever you introduce a new letter, make related alphabet items for the children to take home. For example, for the letter *C* cut out paper cookie shapes and mark them with *C*'s. Place the cookies in a cookie jar and let each child reach in and take one. Other suggestions include marking paper egg shapes with *E*'s, marking play money with *M*'s and marking little party-favor umbrellas with *U*'s.

ABC Bulletin Board

Make a set of large alphabet letters out of posterboard. Let the children work together to decorate the letters by gluing on items whose names begin with the letters. For example, have them glue buttons on the letter *B*, macaroni on the letter *M*, sand on the letter *S* and yarn on the letter *Y*. Arrange the decorated letters on a bulletin board or a wall in alphabetical order.

Letter Prints

Make paint pads by placing folded paper towels in shallow containers and pouring on small amounts of tempera paint. Set out alphabet cookie cutters along with sponges that have been cut into letter shapes. (Or use sponge letters purchased from a craft store.) Let the children make letter prints by dipping the cookie cutters and the sponges into the paint and pressing them on sheets of construction paper.

Variation; Let the children use alphabet rubber stamps and commercial ink pads to make letter prints.

Letter Rubbings

Cut alphabet letters out of sandpaper or posterboard. Attach the letters to a tabletop with loops of tape rolled sticky sides out. Let the children take turns placing pieces of light-weight paper on top of the letters and rubbing across them with crayons.

Cookie Cutter Letters

Give the children balls of playdough to pat or roll out flat. Then let them use alphabet cookie cutters to cut letters out of the playdough. Encourage them to cut out specific letters, their initials or the letters that spell their names.

Variation: Let the children use alphabet cookie cutters to make letter cookies. Use prepared sugar cookie dough or let the children help make cookies from scratch. Bake according to the package or recipe directions.

Letter Recognition Activities

Touch and Match Letters

Choose four or five different alphabet letters. For each letter cut out two small posterboard squares. Use a brush dipped in glue to print the letter on the two cards. Then sprinkle on sand, glitter or rice. When the glue has dried, set out the cards. Let the children trace over the textured letters with their fingers to find the matching pairs.

Extension: Place the textured letter cards in a paper bag. Let the children take turns reaching into the bag and identifying the letters by touch.

Letter Puzzles

Use index cards to make puzzles for the letters of the alphabet. To make each puzzle, print an upper-case letter on the left-hand side of a card and print a matching upper- or lower-case letter on the right-hand side. Then cut the card into two interlocking puzzle pieces. Set out the pieces of several puzzles at a time and let the children take turns putting them together.

Letter Pegboard

Hang peg hooks down a pegboard in two parallel rows. Cut index cards in half. Print upper-case letters on one set of cards and print matching upper- or lower-case letters on another set. Cover the cards with clear self-stick paper and punch a hole in the top of each one. Hang the first set of letter cards on the peg hooks in the left-hand row. Then let the children take turns hanging matching letter cards from the second set on the appropriate peg hooks in the right-hand row. Change the cards on the pegboard each day to review different alphabet letters.

Variation: Instead of using a pegboard and peg hooks, screw cup hooks in two parallel rows down the center of a piece of wood.

Letter Clips

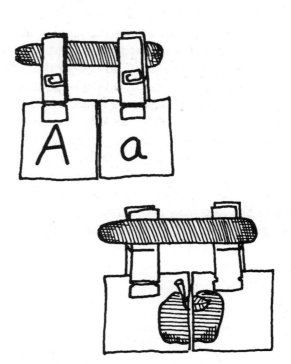

Make a set of clips by gluing two clothespins (2½ inches apart) on a tongue depressor so that the clip ends of the clothespins are hanging down. To make each pair of game cards, fold a small index card in half and print matching alphabet letters on the two halves. Draw a small star in the upper left-hand corner of the index card and another small star in the upper right-hand corner. Turn the card over and draw a simple picture in the center of something whose name begins with the alphabet letter on the card. Then cut the card in half along the fold. Follow the same procedure to make game cards for other letters of the alphabet. To play, have the children clip matching letter cards to the clothespins with the stars in the upper left- and upper right-hand corners. If the matches are correct, the pictures drawn on the backs of the cards will fit together like puzzles.

Letter Gardens

Cut fifteen identical flower shapes out of felt. Choose three alphabet letters such as *A*, *B* and *C*. Label five flowers with *A*'s, five with *B*'s and five with *C*'s. Make an "*A* garden" by placing all the *A* flowers on a flannelboard. Add several *B* and *C* flowers. Then ask the children to "pick" the flowers that do not belong in the *A* garden. Follow the same procedure to make *B* and *C* gardens.

Variation: Place all the flower shapes on the flannelboard and let the children rearrange them to create three separate letter gardens.

Letter Caps

Select a 6-cup muffin tin and six paper baking cups. Print a different upper-case alphabet letter in the bottom of each paper baking cup and place the cups in the muffin tin. Print corresponding lower-case letters on small circles cut from construction paper. Let the children take turns sorting the circles into the appropriate muffin tin cups.

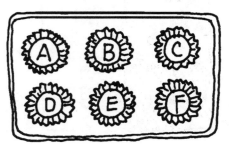

Letter Fish

Cut fish shapes out of construction paper and label them with different alphabet letters. Attach a paper clip to each fish. Make a fishing pole by tying a piece of string to a ruler or a wooden spoon. Tie a magnet on the end of the string. Spread out the fish shapes on the floor. Let the children take turns catching an *G* fish, a *J* fish, a *C* fish, etc.

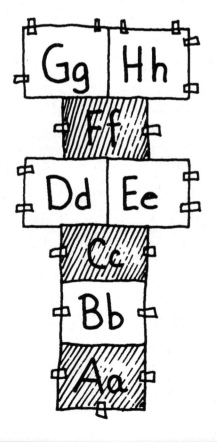

Letter Hopscotch

Print alphabet letters on large posterboard squares. Tape the squares to the floor in a Hopscotch pattern as shown in the illustration. Let the children take turns hopping or stepping from one square to the next. As they do so, have them name the letters on the squares.

Variation: Use chalk to make a letter Hopscotch gameboard on a sidewalk outdoors.

Alphabet Chain

Let the children work together to make an alphabet chain. Set out 51 strips (about 1 by 8 inches each) cut from colored construction paper. Help the children print the letters A to Z on 26 of the strips. Then have them glue the strips together in an alphabet chain, starting with the letter A and alternating a plain strip with the appropriate letter strip. Hang the completed alphabet chain on a wall or a bulletin board.

Variation: Let each child make an alphabet chain of his or her own.

Typewriter Fun

Set out an old typewriter. Insert a sheet of typing paper and invite a child to sit in front of the typewriter with you. Show the child how to type a few alphabet letters. Then let the child try typing letters by him or herself. When the child has finished, remove the paper from the typewriter and help the child name his or her typed letters. Continue in the same manner until each child has had a turn.

Alphabet Block Match

Make game cards by printing individual alphabet letters on small index cards. Or print simple words or the children's names on large index cards. Place the cards and a set of alphabet blocks on a table. Let the children take turns selecting cards and finding alphabet blocks that match the letters on the cards.

Tongue Depressor Puzzles

Choose a familiar three-letter word such as "cat." Place three tongue depressors together side by side on a table. Use a felt-tip marker to print the letters C, A and T on the bottom parts of the three sticks. Then keeping the sticks together, draw a picture of a cat across the top parts of the tongue depressors. Follow the same procedure to make several more puzzles, using words such as "sun," "hat" and "pig." Set out the pieces of the puzzles and let the children have fun putting them together.

Additional Activities

Adapt any of the following activities to make letter games: Shape Mailboxes (page 42); Shape Cubes (page 43); Shape Card Game (page 44); Shape Lotto Game (page 45); Shape Folder (page 45); Shape Sticks (page 46); Concentration (page 47).

Opportunities for Reading and Writing

MAKING LISTS

Supply Lists

Let the children see you making lists of supplies you need for the room or for particular projects. Discuss your lists with the children and ask them to help you think of specific items to include. When your lists are complete, read through them with the group.

Grocery Lists

Let the children help you make lists of foods to buy for special parties or for snacktime cooking projects. Check off the items on the lists as you unpack them.

Repair and Cleaning Lists

Have the children help you make lists of repair and cleaning jobs that need to be done in your room. As you complete the jobs, let the children observe as you check them off your lists.

Playtime Lists

Let the children help you make lists of things they want to do when they go outside to play. Make sure each child gets a chance to contribute to the lists.

Creating Lists

Set out paper, pencils, crayons and felt-tip markers. Encourage the children to draw or "write" lists of their own. For example, they might make lists of their favorite foods, lists of things that are red, list of toys they would like to have or lists of things for which they are thankful.

Variation: Provide the children with picture lists from which they can check off the items they want.

MAKING GROUP BOOKS

Group Telephone Book

Give each child a piece of plain white paper to use for making a book page. Help the children write their names across the tops of their papers and their telephone numbers across the bottoms. Then provide crayons or felt-tip markers and let the children draw self-portraits in the centers of their papers. When the children have finished, put their book pages together, punch holes on the left-hand side and place the pages in a three-ring binder. Encourage the children to use their group telephone book when making calls on a play telephone.

Group Recipe Book

Help each child create a page for a group recipe book. Ask the child to name his or her favorite dish and then tell you how it is prepared. As the child does so, write down a simplified version of his or her recipe (right or wrong) on a piece of paper. Let the children decorate their recipe pages with crayons or felt-tip markers. If desired, cover the pages with clear self-stick paper. Then combine the pages into a group recipe book and place it in your book corner or cooking center. Encourage the children to "read" their recipes to one another.

OFFICE-COMMUNICATIONS CENTER

Creating an Office-Communications Center

Set up a play center for the children in a special area of your room. Fill it with tables and chairs plus a variety of materials that will lead to reading and writing through dramatic play. Below are some suggested materials and props that you might wish to include.

- Pencils
- Pens
- Crayons
- Felt-tip markers
- Pencil holders
- Note pads
- Typing paper
- Lined paper
- Envelopes
- Index cards
- Chalkboard
- Chalk
- Memo board
- Clipboard
- Store catalogs
- Newspapers
- Magazines
- Telephone books
- Cookbooks
- Picture dictionaries
- Play telephones
- Typewriter
- Computer
- Mailbox
- Junk mail
- Letter stencils
- Stamp-type stickers
- Rubber office stamps
- Ink pads

OFFICE-COMMUNICATIONS CENTER ACTIVITIES

Yellow Page Phone Orders

Encourage the children to look through the Yellow Pages of old telephone books to find ads of businesses from which they would like to order things. Have them write down the telephone numbers of the businesses and make pretend lists of things they want to order. Then have them call in their orders on play telephones. For example, they might call pizza parlors with their pizza orders, auto repair shops with their lists of car repairs or toy stores with their lists of toys to be delivered.

Store Catalog Orders

Let the children look through store catalogs and pick out items they want to order. Help them to list their orders on paper, sign them, place them in envelopes and address the envelopes to the catalog company. Then let the children attach stamp-type stickers to their envelopes and mail them in your play center's mailbox.

Variation: Let the children call in their orders on play telephones.

Dictionary Fun

Each day encourage the children to look up words in a children's picture dictionary. Try to choose words that relate to what you are doing that day. For example, if the book you read at storytime is about mice, ask the children to look up the word "mouse."

PLAY CENTERS

Post Office

- Turn your office-communications center into a post office by adding a large "Post Office" sign.

- Set out an extra-large mailbox and additional stamp-type stickers.

- Label shoeboxes with alphabet letters for sorting mail. Print matching letters on junk mail envelopes.

- Let the children take turns being the mail sorter and the stamp seller. Encourage the rest of the children to "write" letters to mail at your post office.

Bank

- Hang a large "Bank" sign in your office-communications center.

- Provide play money along with deposit and withdrawal slips.

- Let several children at a time be tellers. Have the other children be bank customers and pretend to fill out and sign the deposit and withdrawal slips.

Travel Agency

- Label your office-communications center with a large "Travel Agency" sign.

- Decorate the walls of the play center with maps and colorful travel posters.

- Set out travel brochures along with pretend tickets and itinerary forms.

- Let the children take turns being travel agents and pretending to fill out the tickets and itinerary forms for their customers.

PLAY CENTERS

Police Station

- Use a "Police Station" sign to turn your office-communications center into a police station.
- Make simplified versions of traffic tickets and accident forms to place in the play center.
- Let the children take turns being police officers. Have them pretend to fill out the traffic tickets and accident forms during dramatic play.

Doctors' Office

- Display a "Doctors' Office" sign in your office-communications center.
- Provide dress-up props such as white jackets, doctor bags and stethoscopes.
- Set out pads of pretend prescription forms along with brochures outlining good-health habits (eating proper foods, brushing teeth, getting lots of exercise, etc.).
- Let the children take turns being doctors. Have them "write" prescriptions and discuss the good-health brochures with their patients.

Newspaper Office

- Hang a sign that reads "Newspaper Office" in your office-communications center.
- Make press badges for the children to wear.
- Have the children pretend to be reporters and encourage them to "write" stories for their newspaper. Let them carry note pads around during the day, pretending to jot down "hot news items."

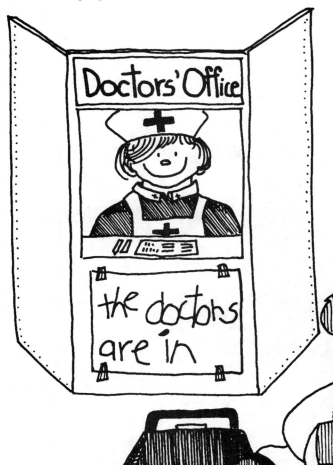

PLAY CENTERS

Home Area

- When the children are playing in the housekeeping area, provide a memo board, a recipe file and writing materials such as note pads, pencils, index cards and envelopes.
- Encourage the children to leave pretend messages (notes or pictures) on the memo board.
- Let the children "read" recipes and make their own pretend recipe cards. Encourage them also to "write" such things as shopping lists and letters to friends or businesses.

Restaurant

- Set up a restaurant play area for the children.
- Let the children help name their restaurant and make a large sign for it.
- Provide real menus or let the children help design menus of their own. Also provide note pads for order taking.
- Let the children take turns being waitpersons and customers. After the customers "read" the menus, have the waitpersons pretend to write down their orders on the note pads.

Garage

- Set up a garage-gas station play area outside where the children can drive in their bikes and wagons for repairs or fill-ups.
- Provide pretend work-order forms attached to clipboards.
- Let the children take turns being garage attendants. When the customers bring in their vehicles, have the garage attendants pretend to make lists of needed repairs on the work-order forms.

PLAY CENTERS

School

- Set up a play school area in your room.
- Provide materials for "reading" and "writing" such as books, pretend worksheets, pencils and paper.
- Let the children take turns being the teacher and helping the students do pretend reading and writing activities. Have the teacher also do such things as check attendance lists, "read" messages from the principal and "write" pretend notes to send home to parents.

Bakery

- Let the children help set up a bakery play area and make a large sign for it.
- Set out playdough, flour and baking utensils such as pans, rolling pins and cookie cutters.
- Provide a recipe file and blank index cards for the bakers. Let them "write" recipes on the cards or have them glue on pictures of baked goods.
- Let the children take turns waiting on customers and pretending to write down orders on small note pads.

Library

- Set up a play library in your book area.
- Provide pretend library cards, paper and pencils, and library brochures listing special events and story hours.
- Let the children take turns being the librarian and doing such things as these: giving out library cards, making pretend lists of books being checked out and checked in, handing out library brochures and "reading" stories to library patrons.

WORDLESS STORIES

Picture Storybook

For this activity you will need a blank photo album with magnetic pages. To make illustrations for the book, cut a variety of pictures out of magazines. Cover the pictures with clear self-stick paper and place them in a box. Invite a child to choose several pictures from the box and help him or her put the pictures in the photo album in any order desired. Then let the child "read" the book to you by making up a story to fit the pictures. Remove the pictures from the photo album and replace them in the box before inviting the next child to have a turn.

WORDLESS STORIES

Sticker Storybook

Collect a three-ring binder and a number of clear plastic page covers to fit inside it. Have on hand identical stickers of one character such as a teddy bear, a duck or a butterfly. Cut full-page pictures out of magazines. Randomly attach a sticker of the same character to each picture. Slide the pictures, back to back, into the plastic page covers and put the pages in the three-ring binder. Invite one child at a time to look through the book with you. Have the child make up a story about the sticker character as it appears on each page of the book.

Variation: Cut small pictures out of magazines and trim them to fit in the pages of a wing-type wallet photo holder. Attach a red self-stick circle to each picture. Put two of the pictures in each of the photo holder pages, picture sides out. Let the children take turns telling the story of the red "bouncing ball" as it moves from page to page.

WORDLESS STORIES

Sequence Book

Make book pages by drawing pictures of a sequence of events on large index cards. For example, to show the growth stages of a pumpkin draw pictures of a seed in the ground, a sprouting seed, a vine with leaves, a vine with flowers, a vine with small green pumpkins and a vine with large orange pumpkins. Cover the book pages with clear self-stick paper. Then put the pages together and punch two holes on the left-hand side. To use the book, mix up the pages and give them to a child, along with two brass paper fasteners. Have the child arrange the pages in the proper sequence and insert the paper fasteners. Then let the child "read" the book to you. Before letting another child use the book, remove the paper fasteners and mix up the pages again.

WORDLESS STORIES

Rubber Stamp Book

For this activity collect a number of rubber stamps, including at least one person or animal character, and several colored ink pads. Make a blank book by putting large index cards together, punching holes on the left-hand side and inserting brass paper fasteners. Use the rubber stamp of a person or animal to print that character on each page of the book. Then turn each page into a simple picture by using the other rubber stamps to create scenes. Let each child have a turn "reading" the book by making up a story about the character that appears on each page.

Variation: Let each child make a rubber stamp book of his or her own.

MAKING BOOKS

Setting Up a Print Shop

Set up a print shop area where the children can create their own original books. Provide materials such as these: white paper, colored construction paper, stapler, hole punch, yarn or ribbon, felt-tip markers, crayons, magazine pictures, construction paper shapes, stickers, rubber stamps, ink pads, scissors and glue.

Making Blank Books

Show the children how to make blank books by putting pieces of white paper together with colored paper covers and stapling the pages together on the left-hand sides. Or help the children punch two holes on the left-hand sides of their books. Then show them how to fasten their book pages together with pieces of yarn or ribbon.

Illustrating Books

Let the children decorate the pages of their blank books by drawing, gluing or stamping on pictures. Help them to print their names and titles on their book covers. Encourage the children to "read" their picture books to you and to one another.

Variation: Occasionally, when a child finishes making a book, write the child's words on the pages as he or she tells you the story.

MAKING BOOKS

"I Like" Books

A simple kind of book that young children enjoy making is called an "I Like" book. First, help each child make a blank book as described on the previous page. On the front cover help the child print the following title, using his or her name in place of "Adam": "Adam's 'I Like' Book." Then help the child print the words "I like" at the top of each page. To complete the book, let the child draw or paste a picture on each page of something that he or she likes. Arrange a special time for the children to "read" their books to one another. Or have them place their books in the library corner for everyone to read.

Hint: Use a copy machine to make copies of pages with the words "I like" printed at the top. Place the pages in your print shop area so that the children can make "I Like" books whenever they wish.

ABC Books

Help each child make a blank book that contains a page for each letter of the alphabet. Print "My ABC Book" and the child's name on the cover. Then label the pages "*A* is for," "*B* is for," "*C* is for," and so on. Have the children work on one page of their books at a time. Give them precut pictures of things whose names begin with the letter on the page. Let them glue on the pictures and add appropriate drawings or picture stickers. Encourage the children to "read" their book pages to you and to one another as they complete them.

GREETING CARDS

Making Greeting Cards

Provide the children with many opportunities to make greeting cards for family members or friends.

- Show the children how to make simple cards by folding pieces of plain paper in half or in fourths. Let the children decorate their cards with such materials as crayons, felt-tip markers, stickers, rubber stamp prints, tissue paper pieces, magazine cutouts or glitter.

- Making holiday greeting cards is an excellent way to get children into the writing habit. Let them use paper and decorative materials in seasonal colors. Pre-writers can easily add messages by using rubber stamps that contain seasonal salutations.

- A favorite card to make for any occasion is the Flap Card, or Surprise Card. Give each child a piece of construction paper. Help the child print a greeting such as "Happy Birthday" or "Merry Christmas" across the top of the paper and his or her name across the bottom. Have the child draw or glue a picture of a surprise gift in the center of the paper. Then help the child glue or tape a flap over the picture. When the recipient gets the card, he or she must peek beneath the flap to find the special surprise.

Variation: Let the children make folded cards with their hidden picture surprise glued inside.

GROUP CORRESPONDENCE

Sending Group Messages

Always be aware of opportunities for having the children create group cards, letters, invitations, and so on.

• Let the children help print salutations on a long piece of shelf paper and then add decorations. Roll up the paper and deliver it to a group member who is sick.

• Help the children make a Hugs and Kisses Chain to let someone know how much you all like him or her. Have the children print O's and X's on paper strips and then glue the strips together to create a giant chain.

• Let the children help you design invitations for an open house or other similar event. Have the children take the invitations home and give them to their parents to read.

• When someone does something nice for your group, let the children help make a giant thank-you card. If desired, print the words "Thank you (person's name)" on the front of the card in large block letters. Let the children decorate the letters as desired and then sign their names inside the card.

• Send away for items as a group so that you will receive group mail to share.

ROOM LABELS

Making Room Labels

Room labels, used in moderation, can provide excellent opportunities for beginning sight-reading activities. Children soon learn that labels are words and that words tell us what things are. Following are some suggestions for using labels in your room.

- Use index cards and felt-tip markers to make labels for a few large objects in your room. For example, print the word "Door" on a card and attach it to one of your doors.

- Label areas where supplies are kept with words such as "Paint," "Paper," "Blocks" and "Books." Help the children learn to read the labels during cleanup time.

- Attach labels to small objects around the room. For example, label paint jars with their color names or label the scissors holder with the word "Scissors."

- Label individual cubbies with the children's names. If you use such things as toothbrushes and drinking glasses in your program, label them with the children's names also.

- Label chairs or seating mats with the children's names. Move the chairs or mats around each day and have the children search for their new places to sit.

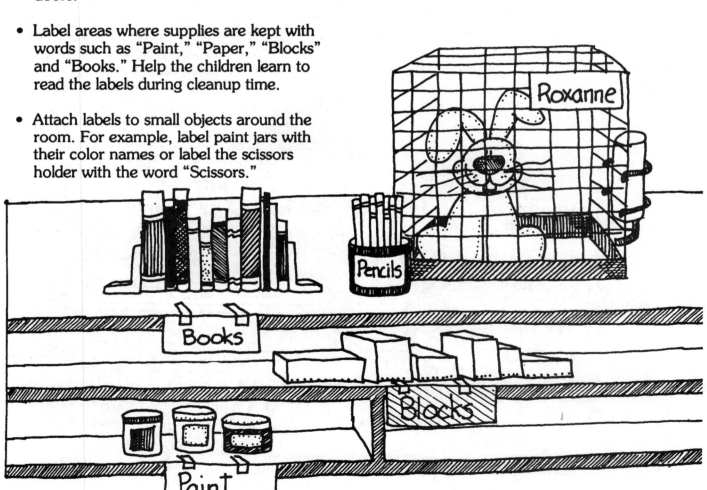

ROOM SIGNS

Making Room Signs

Combine simple words with pictures to create signs for your room. Following are some suggestions to get you started.

- Make a large sign that allows the children to choose which learning areas they wish to play in each day. Cover the sign with clear self-stick paper. Let the children mark their choices with a black crayon. At the end of the day, erase the crayon marks with a soft cloth.

- Create a sign with pockets to use for assigning room monitor duties. Label each pocket with the name of a different duty and print the children's names on index cards to insert in the pockets.

- Create your own calendar to display on a wall in your room. Make sure that the names of the days and the months are printed clearly. Or create a weather calendar to help the children learn such words as "sunny," "rainy" and "cloudy."

- Display signs at the science table that show how to water the plants, feed the animals or do simple experiments.

- Make large signs for such things as fast-food restaurants, gas stations, supermarkets and other kinds of stores. Place the signs in the block area to encourage dramatic play. Or store pieces of cardboard and felt-tip markers in the block area so that you can easily help the children create their own signs.

ROOM MESSAGES

Children's Memo Board

Surprise the children with notes posted on a memo board in a kitchen or office play center. Use simple words and pictures to create messages such as "Snow today!" or "You are special!"

Messages for Parents

Have the children observe as you leave messages for parents on a special memo board near your door. Include short reminders that you could read to the children, if they were curious. For example: "No school on Friday" or "Nature walk next Tuesday." The important thing is to let the children see you using written words to communicate with others.

Safety Messages

Post messages inside or outside your room for safety purposes. For example, after washing the floor, display a sign reading "Watch your step!" Or post a message reading "Keep off!" when a swing or other piece of play equipment become broken.

Trash Can Messages

Let the children help select monthly messages to post on your trash can, such as "Stash your trash!" or "Feed the Paper Monster!" If desired, let the children decorate their messages before attaching them to the trash can.

MESSAGE WHEELS

Making a Message Wheel

Divide a cardboard circle or a paper plate into four to six sections. In the center use a brass paper fastener to hook on a spinner. (Use a large closed safety pin for a spinner or cut an arrow-shaped spinner from a piece of stiff plastic.) Label the sections of the message wheel with different word or picture choices for the children to "read," as suggested in the other activities on this page.

Art Wheel

Print color names in the sections of the message wheel. Let the children use the spinner to select colors to use while painting or drawing.

Story Wheel

Print the titles of favorite books in the message wheel sections. At storytime let a child choose a book for you to read by spinning the spinner.

Game Wheel

Print the names of favorite games in the sections of the message wheel. Let a child choose a game for the group to play by spinning the spinner. Or fill the sections with the children's names. Have the children use the spinner to determine turns or to choose partners.

Movement Wheel

Label the message wheel sections with names and pictures of animals. Let the children choose animals by spinning the spinner. Then have them act out the animals' movements.

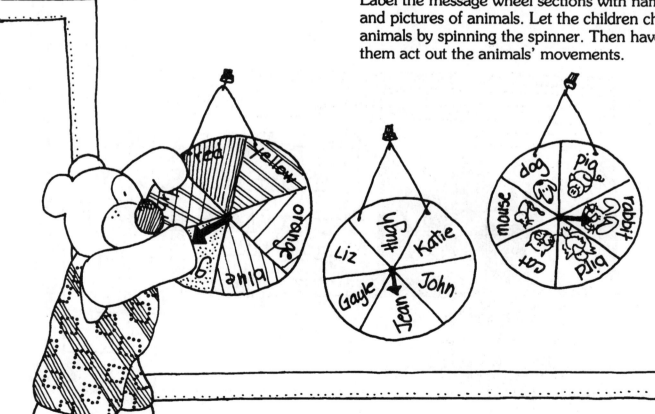

SONG CHARTS

Making a Song Chart

Select a piece of lined chart paper. Or use a chart-sized piece of butcher paper or posterboard and draw on faint guidelines with a pencil. With a black felt-tip marker print the words to a familiar childhood song on your chart. Use upper- and lower-case letters as shown in the illustration. Hang the chart on a wall or an easel and invite the children to sit in front of it. Then sing the song with them, pointing to each word on the chart as you sing it. Follow the same procedure to make charts for as many favorite songs as you wish.

RHYME CHARTS

Making a Rhyme Chart

Choose a favorite nursery rhyme and print it on a lined chart. (See the directions for making a song chart on the previous page). Let the children decorate the top and bottom of the chart with crayon drawings or prints made with sponge shapes dipped in tempera paint. Display the chart where the children can easily see it. Let them have fun "reading" the rhyme with you as you move your finger under the printed lines on the chart.

Extension: After you have made charts for a number of nursery rhymes, put together small books containing copies of the rhymes for the children to enjoy "reading" on their own.

DICTATING STORIES

Creating Original Stories

Encourage the children to make up stories about pictures they have drawn, their play experiences or any topics that spark their imaginations. Invite one child at a time to tell you his or her story as you write down the words. Read back each sentence as the story is formulated to help the child continue. When the child has finished, read back his or her entire story in a natural speaking tone, pointing to the words as you say them. (This helps the child understand the relationship between speaking and writing.) If the children wish to share their dictated stories, plan to read them aloud at circle time.

Note: When the children are dictating their stories, be sure to write down their exact words. The purpose of this activity is not to teach grammar but to help the children see that their spoken words can be translated into written words which can then be read over and over again.

Extension: For each child save stories dictated at the beginning of the year and compare them with those dictated at the end of the year. Notice the sense of confidence and the improved vocabulary in the later stories.

DICTATING SONGS

Creating Original Songs

At circle time encourage the children to make up group Piggyback songs, or songs that can be sung to familiar tunes. To get the children started, help them decide on a song topic and on some of the things they want their song to say. Together, choose a tune from a familiar song such as one of those listed below. Then work with the children to write a new song to go with the tune. Print the words of each new song on a separate song chart to display in your room (see page 124). Let the children have fun singing their own original songs as they "read" the words on the charts.

- "Frere Jacques"
- "Mary Had a Little Lamb"
- "Row, Row, Row Your Boat"
- "Jingle Bells"
- "Did You Ever See a Lassie?"
- "I'm a Little Teapot"
- "The Farmer in the Dell"
- "The Muffin Man"
- "Twinkle, Twinkle, Little Star"

We Love Noodles
Sung to: "Frere Jacques"

We love noodles, we love noodles

In our soup, in our soup.

Slippery, slurpy noodles,

Slippery, slurpy noodles.

In our soup.

In our soup.

STORY MAT

Making a Story Mat

Use a 12- by 18-inch piece of blue construction paper to make a two-sided story mat. Create a "summer scene" on one side by gluing on a grassy hill shape cut from green construction paper. Then turn the mat over and glue on a snowy hill shape cut from white construction paper for a "winter scene." Cover both sides of the story mat with clear self-stick paper.

Using the Story Mat

- Cut out paper shapes (or pictures) of people, animals, trees, clouds, toys, etc. Include seasonal summer and winter shapes as well. Place all the shapes in a "story box."

- Let the children take turns choosing shapes they want from the box. Encourage them to tell stories as they manipulate the paper shapes on the summer or winter story mat.

- If desired, tape-record the children's stories for sharing at circle time or for later transcription by an adult.

FLANNELBOARD

Making a Flannelboard

Select an extra-large piece of heavy cardboard. Using strong glue or tape, cover the cardboard with a piece of felt or heavy flannel. (Choose a color such as blue that can serve as an all-purpose background.) Stand your flannelboard on a chair seat, in an easel tray or against a wall.

Using the Flannelboard

- Cut story characters and shapes out of felt. Or cut out pictures or paper shapes and back them with strips of felt or sandpaper. Keep a box of miscellaneous characters and shapes available at all times for creating stories.

- Place felt characters on your flannelboard as you tell the children a story. Then let the children use the characters to retell the story or to make up new stories.

- Have the children work together to make up a story. Let them take turns choosing a felt character, placing it on the flannelboard and incorporating it into their group story.

- If desired, preserve the children's stories by recording them on tape.

MAGNETBOARD FUN

Magnetboards

Use a cookie sheet, a pizza pan, a refrigerator door or any other metallic surface for a magnetboard. Or magnetize your flannelboard by placing a piece of fine-mesh wire screen between the felt or flannel and the cardboard backing.

Magnetic Letter Activities

Purchase several sets of magnetic alphabet letters (available at toy stores). Use the letters with a magnetboard for the activities that follow.

- Encourage the children to group like letters.

- Spell out simple messages for the children to "read."

- Help the children spell out their names or simple words.

- Spell out opposites such as "hot" and "cold" or "big" and "little." glue pictures illustrating the concepts on small cards and back the cards with pieces of magnetic tape. Have the children place the pictures under the appropriate words.

- Print simple words on strips of posterboard and glue pieces of magnetic tape to the backs. Place the strips on a magnetboard. Have the children find matching magnetic letters and place them below the printed letters.

PHOTOS WITH CAPTIONS

Printed Photo Captions

Take or collect different kinds of photographs as suggested below. Mount the photos on pieces of heavy paper. Let the children help you think up simple captions for the photos. Have them observe as you print the captions beneath the pictures. Then display the photos around the room and encourage the children to "read" the captions.

- Photos of individual children or family members.
- Photos of toys or other familiar objects.
- Photos of play areas.
- Photos of familiar places.
- Photos of field trips, parties or other group happenings.

Magnetic Letter Photo Captions

On separate cards mount individual photos of familiar people, animals or objects. Print the names of the photo subjects on the cards. Then cover the cards with clear self-stick paper and tape them to a refrigerator or other metallic surface. Give a child a container of magnetic letters. Below each photo card have the child use magnetic letters to copy the name that is printed on the card.

Hint: If doing this activity at home, use photos of family members.

RESOURCE MATERIALS FROM HOME

Collecting Resource Materials

When working with young children, your best source for reading and writing materials is from the home. Try collecting the following materials to use with your group:

- Junk mail for the children to open, "read" and sort through.

- Souvenir picture postcards from around the world.

- "Important day" newspapers for reading and discussing at circle time.

- Old magazines to cut up and use for art projects or for letter and word recognition games.

- Letters of commendation or certificates of merit.

- Old picture books and storybooks to add to your reading corner.

- Outdated address or office stamps to use for printing words and phrases.

- Favorite recipes printed on index cards for placing in your cooking center.

TAPE RECORDINGS

Tape Recorder Activities

Keep a tape recorder in your room to use for activities such as the ones that follow.

- **Record familiar sounds** (a telephone ringing, a dog barking, a car horn honking, etc.). Play back the tape and ask the children to identify the sounds they hear.

- **Record different kinds of messages** to play for the children (good-morning messages, safety messages, special announcements, etc.).

- **Record simple movement directions** for the children to follow. For example: "Stand up straight; Bend down low; Wiggle your body; Tap your toe."

- Record simple songs and rhymes on tape. Use the tapes with song and rhyme charts (see pages 124 and 125).

- Record the children's voices when they are making up original stories. Keep the tapes to share at circle time.

- Use commercial story tapes to help the children see the relationship between the spoken word and the printed word. Or make your own story tapes using favorite books from your reading corner. Show the children how they can follow the words in a storybook while listening to the accompanying tape.

STORY CHARTS

Making and Using a Story Chart

Choose any of the activity ideas on these two pages for making a story chart. Use a black felt-tip marker to print your story on a piece of lined chart paper or a sheet of plain posterboard on which you have drawn faint guidelines with a pencil. Attach your story chart to a wall or an easel where the children can easily see it. Then read the story many times with the group, pointing to the words as you read them. Keep the chart posted in your room so that you and the children can reread the story often.

Special Event Story Chart

Let the children help you make a story chart after a major group event such as a trip to a fire station, a Valentine's Day party or a demonstration given by a special class visitor. Use the children's words to describe what happened during the event.

Fairy Tale or Folktale Story Chart

Ask the children to choose a favorite fairy tale or folktale such as "The Three Bears" or "Little Red Riding Hood." Make a story chart by writing down the children's version of the tale.

End-Of-Day Story Chart

Just before the children go home, let them help you write a group story about what they did that day. Encourage them to tell about the games they played, the songs they sang, what they ate for a snack, etc.

The Pig
Today a pig came to school. We fed the pig. He ate carrots.

STORY CHARTS

Seasonal Story Chart

Let the children touch and examine items placed on a seasonal science table. Encourage them to make up a story about the items. As they tell their story, write it down on a piece of chart paper or butcher paper.

Wordless Book Story Chart

After sharing a wordless storybook with the children, make copies of the pictures and attach them in the proper sequence to a piece of chart paper. Go through the pictures with the children. Beneath each one, write down a group version of what is happening in the picture. When you have finished, read the story back to the children so that they can hear their words while looking at the pictures.

Newspaper Story Chart

Cut interesting photographs from old newspapers and attach them to a sheet of chart paper. Let the children help you write short captions for the photos, such as "Firefighter Saves Cat" or "Giant Watermelon Wins Prize at Fair."

"We Like" Story Chart

Title a piece of chart paper "Foods We Like." (Or choose any similar category such as Animals, Toys or Games.) Ask the children to name their favorite foods. As they do so, write down their responses as follows:

"I like meatballs," said Jason.

"I like ice cream," said Katie.

"I like pizza," said Andy.

COMMERCIAL SIGNS

Reading Commercial Signs

Among the first thing that children learn to read are signs for different businesses. These signs are often accompanied by graphic symbols which help young children identify the signs and remember what the signs say. (McDonald's golden arches are an example.) Take advantage of this natural interest in signs to help develop your children's reading skills. Below are a few suggestions.

• Make large cardboard signs that contain words and graphic symbols for well-known businesses (fast-food restaurants, pizza parlors, supermarkets, gas stations, etc.). Place the signs in your block area. Let the children play with the signs as they build replicas of the businesses represented by the signs.

• Make general signs for the children to play with in the block area. Some suggestions would be these: "Bakery, Shoe Shop, Ice Cream Parlor, Drugstore, Post Office, Fire Station."

• Print signs that give directions on pieces of cardboard. Let the children use the signs while playing with toy people and cars in the block area. Include signs such as these: "Keep Off the Grass; Park Here; Stop; Don't Walk; One Way; Exit."

COMMERCIAL LABELS

Reading Commercial Labels

Collect a number of different food boxes and cans that are labeled with familiar brand names ("Campbell's," "Kellogg's," "Chef Boyardee," etc.). For each brand name, include several food containers. Set out the containers to use for the activities that follow.

- Help the children identify and read the brand names on the different containers. Then let them sort the containers into groups according to brand name.

- Cut three or four different brand names out of food containers. Glue the brand names on separate index cards. Set out the cards along with food containers that are labeled with matching brand names. Let the children take turns choosing a card, reading the brand name on it and then finding a food container with a matching brand name.

- Make a book of brand name labels cut from different food containers (or from magazine pictures.) Place the book in your library corner for the children to enjoy "reading."

READING TO CHILDREN

Developing a Love of Reading

One of the most important activities you can do with young children is to read to them. Take advantage of your children's natural interest in hearing what words say and enjoy with them the pleasure that this activity can bring. Following are just a few suggestions for making reading aloud a part of your program.

- At circle time choose favorite books to reread often to your group. Children enjoy hearing familiar stories and anticipating what happens next.

- Let the children take turns choosing a book for you to read each day. When storytime is over, place the book in your library corner so that the children can enjoy looking at it on their own.

- Let the children see you enjoying reading different kinds of written materials. Whenever they express interest, read to them from newspapers, magazines, brochures, cookbooks, etc.

- Take trips to the library with your children. Read aloud short passages from books the children seem interested in. Or visit at a time when the librarian is planning to read stories aloud. Allow the children to choose one or two books to check out and bring back to the room.

READING TO CHILDREN

Story Stretchers

Make storytime more fun and meaningful for your children by using any of the extended activity ideas below.

- When you are reading a familiar storybook, take time to let the children act out what is happening in the story.

- Provide the children with simple props that will encourage them to reenact a familiar story on their own during playtime.

- Pause occasionally while reading a familiar story to talk about what is happening and why.

- When you have finished reading a story, go back and recap the beginning, the middle and the end.

- Encourage the children to tell their own version of a favorite story.

- After reading a story, follow up by reading another story that relates to it in some way. For example, read "The Three Little Pigs" and follow up with a story about pigs on the farm or a story about houses.

CHILDREN READING BOOKS

Books for Oral Reading

Provide the children with different kinds of books that will encourage them to "read" out loud. Following are a few suggestions.

- Obtain copies of wordless picture books from your local children's library. Or make your own wordless books using any of the ideas on pages 112 to 115. Let the children read these books by making up stories about what they think is happening in the pictures.

- Collect a variety of simple storybooks that contain both words and pictures. Read the books aloud many times until the children become familiar with the stories. Invite the children to choose books from the collection to "read" to you or to the group. As they tell the stories, have them use the pictures to help them remember what happens first, next, and so on.

- Even very young children can enjoy reading "repetition and rhyme" books, which can be found at your local children's library. In these books the stories follow the pictures exactly, with lots of repetition and rhyme, and all new words are introduced through the illustrations. Choose one of these books to share with your group. After reading it through once or twice, you will probably find that the children can successfully "read" it on their own.

CHILDREN READING BOOKS

Silent Reading Areas

Children often enjoy looking through books by themselves in a private relaxed atmosphere. Set up a comfortable reading area in a corner of your room. Supply it with lots of pillows and keep it well stocked with both new picture books and old favorites. Or use one of the suggestions that follow to create a special reading spot for your children to share.

- Arrange bookshelves or other pieces of furniture near a wall to form a private reading nook.

- Place an old couch in a corner of the room to be used only for reading books.

- Create a "reading tub" by filling an old bathtub with pillows.

- Set up a small tent in which one or two children at a time can enjoy looking through books.

- Consider building a small reading loft in an appropriate area of your room.

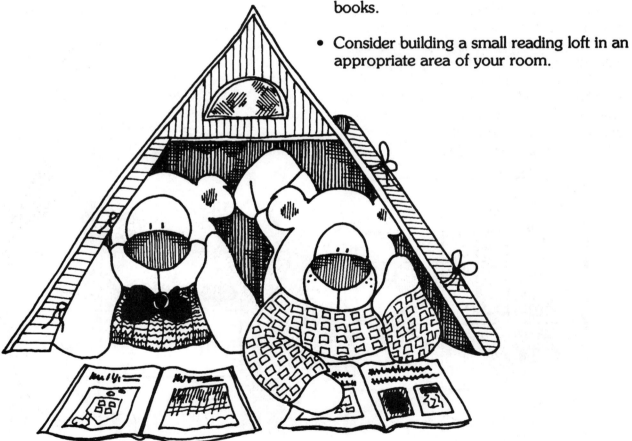

GROUP SURVEYS, CHARTS AND GRAPHS

Learning Areas Survey

Make a survey form to use for discovering how many children worked in each learning area during the day. Draw pictures identifying the different learning areas in your room on a sheet on paper. Then attach the form to a clipboard. Just before the children go home, pass around the survey form and let each child check the learning areas in which he or she worked that day. Read aloud the results of your survey before everyone leaves.

More Survey Fun

Make forms for the children to use for conducting their own surveys. To make each form, print a survey question at the top of a piece of paper. For example: "What is your favorite kind of ice cream? What color shoes are you wearing? What kinds of pets do you have? What color is your hair?" Down the left-hand side of the paper, draw and label pictures that show the most likely responses to the question. Attach the forms to clipboards and hand them out. Let the children interview one another and record answers to the survey questions by making check marks next to the pictures on their survey forms. Later, arrange a time for the children to share the results of their surveys.

Opportunities for Reading and Writing

GROUP SURVEYS, CHARTS AND GRAPHS

Charts and Graphs

Let the children help make charts and graphs like those suggested below.

- At the beginning of each week, make a chart to record the weather. Let the children add appropriate weather symbols to the chart each day.

- When the children are doing a gardening project such as planting seeds, let them help you create a pictorial growth chart. Print appropriate labels on the chart before displaying it in the science area.

- Make and display a chart showing the phases of the moon.

- Make a chart on which the children can write their estimates of how many dried beans there are in a jar or how many seeds there are in a pumpkin. Later, help the children count the beans or seeds and compare the number with their estimates.

- Help the children measure the lengths of different objects, such as a box, a table, a jump rope and a rug. Then record the lengths of the objects on a simple bar graph.

- After the children conduct surveys like those described on the previous page, let them help you create bar graphs to record their survey results.

How many seeds are in the pumpkin

Ann	16	Wendy	20
Fred	70	Doug	57
Peggy	41	Marion	33
Al	36	Steve	85
Hazel	100	Al R.	60

ACTION STORIES

Illustrating Actions

Have the children sit on the floor or around a table. Provide them with crayons and large sheets of paper. Tell the children a simple action story. As you do so, have them draw lines on their papers to illustrate the movements of the different actions. Below are some examples of action sentences along with lines that could be drawn to illustrate them. Encourage the children to make up their own action stories to illustrate, if desired.

The clouds rolled across the sky.

The grass popped up.

The cars raced around the track.

The rain fell down.

The smoke curled up.

The windshield wipers went back and forth.

The worm wiggled through the mud.

The bunny hopped along the trail.

Opportunities for Reading and Writing

SYMBOL STORIES

Decoding Symbol Stories

Decoding symbol stories encourages children to use their imaginations. Use symbols such as circles, squares and wavy lines to create simple "story lines." Have the children assign a word to each symbol. Then let them decode the stories however they wish, using additional words between the symbols to connect the story ideas. For example, write out the following symbol story for the children:

One child might "read" the story something like this: "The mother bear and the baby bear ran down to the lake. They caught three fish and took them home." Another child might read the symbol story something like this: "The truck and the car drove over the mountain and stopped at a big town. They stayed three days and then went home." Start by writing short one-line stories. Then gradually create longer symbol stories like the ones in the illustration for your children to have fun decoding.

SNACKTIME FUN

Reading and Writing at Snacktime

Snacktime offers many opportunities for reading and writing. Following are several suggestions you might wish to consider.

- Make and label a simple picture chart that shows how to set a table. Display the chart in your snack area where the children can easily see it.

- Post a chart that lists which children are to be snack servers for the day.

- Print the children's names on construction paper placemats. Help the children read the names to find their places at the snack table.

- Make construction paper placemats containing a list of food choices for the day. Let the children check off the items they would like to have.

- Print simple words or messages on construction paper placemats. Cover the placemats with clear self-stick paper. While the children are waiting to be served their snacks, let them trace over the words on their placemats with crayons. (To remove the crayon marks, wipe the placemats with a soft cloth.)

SNACKTIME FUN

Preparing Snacks

Make reading and writing a part of snack preparation by using any of the ideas below.

- Let the children help you write shopping lists for special snacktimes or parties. Read back the lists, then take the children to the store with you, if possible. Let the children help check off items on the lists as you purchase them or as you unpack them later.

- Make and display simple picture charts that show how to prepare foods for use in recipes. Include such tasks as washing peeling, cutting and chopping.

- Print labels such as "Sugar," "Flour" or "Macaroni" on food containers that you use for storing staples.

- Before preparing a recipe, print it on a piece of chart paper or butcher paper attached to a wall or an easel. Read through the recipe with the group. Or make a picture chart showing how to prepare the recipe that the children can "read" by themselves.

- When preparing group snacks, make simple charts showing the different duties that need to be done. Help the children write their names next to the duties they choose or have been assigned.

NEWSPAPER FUN

First Editions

Cut interesting photographs, simple headlines
and columns of text out of old newspapers.
Give each child a large piece of plain newsprint or other kind of white paper. Let the
children glue or paste the newspaper photos,
headlines and columns on their papers any
way they wish to create their own paste-ups of
newspaper pages.

Search and Find

Give each child a page from a newspaper and
a crayon or a felt-tip marker. Then ask the
children to search for such things as these:

- The longest word they can find.
- The biggest (in size) word they can find.
- A particular letter such as *B*.
- A particular word such as "and."
- The letters in their own names.

NEWSPAPER FUN

Reading Picture Ads

Cut picture ads from newspapers and mount them on heavy paper. At circle time let each child in turn choose an ad and tell what he or she thinks the ad is selling. Accept all responses.

Sequencing Comics

Cut appropriate comic strips from newspapers and cover them with clear self-stick paper. Read the strips to the children. Then cut the strips into sections and mix them up. Let the children arrange the sections in the proper sequence and tell you what the comic strips "say."

Can You Guess?

- Choose an appropriate newspaper story to share with the children. Read aloud the first part of the story and let the children try guessing how it ends.

- Read just the headline of a newspaper story to the children. See if they can guess what the story is about.

- Read aloud the first part of an appropriate comic strip. Encourage the children to guess how it ends.

BIG BOOKS

Using Big Books

Big Books (enlarged versions of regular-sized books) are ideal for using at storytime to help children become more involved in the language process. As you read the text and move your finger under the lines of print, the children can clearly see the words and observe how they progress from left to right. Look for Big-Book versions of favorite stories at children's bookstores or school supply stores.

Making Big Books

Create your own Big Books using such things as favorite songs or rhymes or your children's dictated stories. Make pages by using a black felt-tip marker to print the desired text on extra-large sheets of paper. Let the children help add illustrations. Before binding your Big Book pages together with heavy paper covers, laminate them or cover them with clear self-stick paper for durability.

Variation: Make Big-Book versions of commercially printed materials for your personal classroom use. Copy the text and illustrations on extra-large sheets of paper. Or, if available, use an opaque projector to enlarge the text and pictures for tracing. (For Totline resources that can be used for making Big Books, see the section that begins on page 153.)

Totline Resources

Teaching Pre-Reading and Pre-Writing Skills With Totline Books

1•2•3 Reading & Writing offers many ideas for providing young children with pre-reading and pre-writing experiences. To implement and expand these ideas, look for additional materials and activities in the Totline books described on these two pages.

1•2•3 ART — Filled with creative open-ended art activities. Great for helping develop pre-writing skills.

1•2•3 PUPPETS — Over 60 simple puppets to make for teaching basic concepts or creating language opportunities. Ideal to use for expanding vocabulary and helping children develop listening skills.

1•2•3 GAMES — Contains open-ended "no-lose" games, many providing language and listening opportunities.

PIGGYBACK SONG BOOKS — Filled with original songs to sing to the tunes of childhood favorites. A number of titles are available, offering lots of rhyme and repetition. Great resources to use for making song charts or Big Books.

THEME-A-SAURUS and **THEME-A-SAURUS II** — Filled with rhymes, songs, concept learning games and lots of language and listening opportunities.

ALPHABET THEME-A-SAURUS — Also filled with rhymes, songs, learning games and language and listening opportunities, all centered around beginning letter recognition. Special features include puppet patterns for each alphabet letter plus alphabet card patterns that can be used for making learning games, room decorations or alphabet books.

"CUT & TELL" SCISSOR STORIES — Each book contains eight original stories with directions for making unique character cutouts from paper plates. Perfect for helping develop listening and language skills. Children love repeating the stories over and over again as you cut out additional characters, thus strengthening their skills in recalling, sequencing and storytelling.

"TAKE-HOME" BOOKS — Repetition and rhyme form the basis of these books. The stories are designed to be easily remembered so that even very young children can successfully "read" them at home. Ideal for building self-esteem in non-readers and beginning readers alike. Excellent resources for making Big Books.

TOTLINE TEACHING TALES — *Teeny-Tiny Folktales* and *Short-Short Stories* offer easy-to-understand stories for reading aloud plus suggestions for expansion into other curriculum areas. *Mini-Mini Musicals* contains stories for young children to sing and re-sing. Great for developing memory, recall and comprehension skills.

1001 PROPS — Chock-full of ideas for inexpensive, easy-to-make teaching aids, many stressing basic learning concepts, letter and word recognition, and likes and differences.

1·2·3 STORIES, RHYMES & SONGS — A collection of open-ended language activities for young children. Great for building language skills and self-esteem.

Notes:

Notes:

Early Learning Resources

Songs, activities, themes, recipes, and tips

Celebrations

Easy, practical ideas for celebrating holidays and special days around the world. Plus ideas for making ordinary days special.

Celebrating Likes and Differences
Small World Celebrations
Special Day Celebrations
Great Big Holiday Celebrations

Theme-A-Saurus®

Classroom-tested, around-the-curriculum activities organized into imaginative units. Great for implementing child-directed programs.

Multisensory Theme-A-Saurus
Theme-A-Saurus
Theme-A-Saurus II
Toddler Theme-A-Saurus
Alphabet Theme-A-Saurus
Nursery Rhyme Theme-A-Saurus
Storytime Theme-A-Saurus

1•2•3 Series

Open-ended, age-appropriate, cooperative, and no-lose experiences for working with preschool children.

1•2•3 Art
1•2•3 Games
1•2•3 Colors
1•2•3 Puppets
1•2•3 Reading & Writing
1•2•3 Rhymes, Stories & Songs
1•2•3 Math
1•2•3 Science
1•2•3 Shapes

Snacks Series

Easy, educational recipes for healthy eating and expanded learning.

Super Snacks
Healthy Snacks
Teaching Snacks
Multicultural Snacks

Piggyback® Songs

New songs sung to the tunes of childhood favorites. No music to read! Easy for adults and children to learn. Chorded for guitar or autoharp.

Piggyback Songs
More Piggyback Songs
Piggyback Songs for Infants & Toddlers
Piggyback Songs in Praise of God
Piggyback Songs in Praise of Jesus
Holiday Piggyback Songs
Animal Piggyback Songs
Piggyback Songs for School
Piggyback Songs to Sign
Spanish Piggyback Songs
More Piggyback Songs for School

Busy Bees

These seasonal books help two- and three-year-olds discover the world around them through their senses. Each book includes fun activity and learning ideas, songs, snack ideas, and more!

Busy Bees—SPRING
Busy Bees—SUMMER
Busy Bees—FALL
Busy Bees—WINTER

101 Tips for Directors

Great ideas for managing a preschool or daycare. These hassle-free, handy hints are a great help.

Staff and Parent Self-Esteem
Parent Communication
Health and Safety
Marketing Your Center
Resources for You and Your Center
Child Development Training

101 Tips for Toddler Teachers

Designed for adults who work with toddlers.

Classroom Management
Discovery Play
Dramatic Play
Large Motor Play
Small Motor Play
Word Play

101 Tips for Preschool Teachers

Valuable, fresh ideas for adults who work with young children.

Creating Theme Environments
Encouraging Creativity
Developing Motor Skills
Developing Language Skills
Teaching Basic Concepts
Spicing Up Learning Centers

Problem Solving Safari

Designed to help children problem-solve and think for themselves. Each book includes scenarios from children's real play and possible solutions.

Problem Solving Safari—Art
Problem Solving Safari—Blocks
Problem Solving Safari—Dramatic Play
Problem Solving Safari—Manipulatives
Problem Solving Safari—Outdoors
Problem Solving Safari—Science

The Best of Totline® Series

Collections of some of the finest, most useful material published in *Totline Magazine* over the years.

The Best of Totline
The Best of Totline Parent Flyers

Totline products are available at fine parent and teacher stores. For the dealer nearest you, call 1-800-421-5565.

Early Learning Resources
Posters, puzzles, and books for parents and children

A Year of Fun

Age-specific books detailing how young children grow and change and what parents can do to lay a foundation for later learning.

Just for Babies
Just for Ones
Just for Twos
Just for Threes
Just for Fours
Just for Fives

Getting Ready for School

Fun, easy-to-follow ideas for developing essential skills that preschoolers need before they can successfully achieve higher levels of learning.

Ready to Learn Colors, Shapes, and Numbers
Ready to Write and Develop Motor Skills
Ready to Read
Ready to Communicate
Ready to Listen and Explore the Senses

Learning Everywhere

Everyday opportunities for teaching children about language, art, science, math, problem solving, self-esteem, and more!

Teaching House
Teaching Town
Teaching Trips

Beginning Fun With Art

Introduce young children to the fun of art while developing coordination skills and building self-confidence.

Craft Sticks • Crayons • Felt
Glue • Paint • Paper Shapes
Modeling Dough • Yarn
Tissue Paper • Scissors
Rubber Stamps • Stickers

Beginning Fun With Science

Make science fun with these quick, safe, easy-to-do activities that lead to discovery and spark the imagination.

Bugs & Butterflies
Plants & Flowers
Magnets
Rainbows & Colors
Sand & Shells
Water & Bubbles

Teaching Tales

Each of these children's books includes a delightful story plus related activity ideas that expand on the story's theme.

Kids Celebrate the Alphabet
Kids Celebrate Numbers

Seeds for Success™

For parents who want to plant the seeds for success in their young children

Growing Creative Kids
Growing Happy Kids
Growing Responsible Kids
Growing Thinking Kids

Learn With Piggyback® Songs

BOOKS AND TAPES
Age-appropriate songs that help children learn!

Songs & Games for Babies
Songs & Games for Toddlers
Songs & Games for Threes
Songs & Games for Fours

Learning Puzzles

Designed to challenge as children grow.

Kids Celebrate Numbers
Kids Celebrate the Alphabet
Bear Hugs 4-in-1 Puzzle Set
Busy Bees 4-in-1 Puzzle Set

Two-Sided Circle Puzzles

Double-sided, giant floor puzzles designed in a circle with cutout pieces for extra learning and fun.

Underwater Adventure
African Adventure

We Work & Play Together Posters

A colorful collection of cuddly bear posters showing adult and children bears playing and working together.

We Build Together
We Cook Together
We Play Together
We Read Together
We Sing Together
We Work Together

Bear Hugs® Health Posters

Encourage young children to develop good health habits. Additional learning activities on back!

We Brush Our Teeth
We Can Exercise
We Cover our Coughs and Sneezes
We Eat Good Food
We Get Our Rest
We Wash Our Hands

Reminder Posters

Photographic examples of children following the rules.

I cover my coughs
I listen quietly
I pick up my toys
I put my things away
I say please and thank you
I share
I use words when I am angry
I wash my hands
I wipe my nose

Totline products are available at fine parent and teacher stores. For the dealer nearest you, call 1-800-421-5565.

If you like Totline® Books, you'll love Totline® Magazine!

For fresh ideas that challenge and engage young children in active learning, reach for **Totline Magazine**—Proven ideas from innovative teachers!

Each issue includes

- Seasonal learning themes
- Stories, songs, and rhymes
- Open-ended art projects
- Science explorations
- Reproducible parent pages
- Ready-made teaching materials
- Activities just for toddlers
- Reproducible healthy snack recipes
- Special pull-outs

Receive a free copy of Totline® Magazine by calling 800-609-1724 for subscription information.

VILLA PARK PUBLIC LIBRARY